Christmas, 1977

To our goyische friend —

Good luck.

Phil

The disadvantages of signing
second are herein made
apparent. We love you.

Ellen

A BOOK
OF PARABLES

Also by Daniel Berrigan

No One Walks Waters
Consequences, Truth and
Night Flight to Hanoi
They Call Us Dead Men
False Gods, Real Men
Dark Night of Resistance
Trial of the Catonsville Nine
America is Hard to Find
Jesus Christ
Prison Poems
Selected and New Poems
Lights on in the House of the Dead

A BOOK
OF PARABLES

Daniel Berrigan

A Crossroad Book
The Seabury Press · New York

1977
The Seabury Press
815 Second Avenue
New York, N.Y. 10017

Quotations from the Holy Scriptures are from *The Jerusalem Bible.*

Printed in the United States of America

Library of Congress Cataloging In Publication Data

Berrigan, Daniel.   A Book of Parables
"A Crossroad book."
1. Bible. O.T.—Meditations. I. Title.
BS1151.5.B47   242   76-53537   ISBN 0-8164-0328-7

FRIDA BERRIGAN
1886–1976

There
on the shore
Jesus
stood.
And
it was morning.

CONTENTS

Preface

The genesis of this was a season both scalding and chilling in Detroit. I was living in the ghetto there, teaching at the University and taking care of my landlord. He was an ancient Greek seer, dying of cancer; his description is given in the part called "Patience of Job in Detroit."

It was Lent outside and within. I thought that a meditation on certain episodes of the Old Testament might lighten the mood. A kind of dance in and out, ordered and spontaneous, irreverent and at times fierce, through the human condition.

The manuscript has had an interesting life already. I was told at one time that it was too angry for good use; at another, that it was scandalous. It seems to me that both anger and scandal are in the eye of the beholder. Plank or mote, it's their problem, as the cliché goes.

I love the book like an errant child. I am, after all, responsible for it; but so is God, who has a certain responsibility not only for the book, but for its author as well. Let him look to it; I have.

There is also something to be said for the struggle of living a life, writing a book. I believe the classical expression is "wrestling with God." In that skill He is skillful beyond bearing. But he has not won yet, and I am still around, between bouts. I have a feeling he is too; which probably separates me from his pallbearers of the middle sixties. Their obituary, I believe, was premature. (This statement is called, in the old manuals, and indeed in the bible, faith. I am inordinately glad to say this.)

The book is an attempt to take discourse out of the civilized parlor, where it so often groans and faints like a Dickens heroine (big on swoons, mousey on outcry), into the arena where sweat and perhaps even blood run freely. I wanted to find out for myself, so to speak, whether Job was right or his friends. Should God be talked to, or about? If the second, he is condemned to the sidelines, a mute observer of the human frenzy and folly; but if the first, we are in trouble, certainly, and in hope, probably. Maybe in troubled hope. The author lives in troubled hope. That's why he talks that way, angry, as they say, and scandalous.

But will the friends of the author, who find him scandalous, take another look at the friends of Job? And then another look at Job? They are, I believe, reputable theologians; but he is something else again.

Maybe, in fact, given the church today and its spokespeople, we ought to declare the book intolerable, I mean the Book of Job; too angry in parts, too scandalous in others. And then, from the depths of our swoons and stuffy parlors, write another: the Book of the Friends of Job. That would sit better with practically everybody. We could all squat in a circle and talk about God while the unsavory, skinny figure in our midst undergoes him. That would finally make sense.

I love the book. Is that allowed? With a kiss of the hand I present the first copy—to Job.

Daniel Berrigan

Eve and the
Bible Salesman

In the beginning there was no necessity.

This is known as the intellectual long way round; invented by philosophers, who learned the reasoning and method from a stone; known thereafter as the philosopher's stone, naturally. What they mean to say is, once there were no rules. What that means is hard to say, something outside the story, outside the mind, outside possibility. Rule ridden now, we come after.

I was interested particularly in *her* mind. It seemed to have the exact, monochromatic character of the story itself. Unreflecting. A woman, a man, in a house in a clearing, where the trees brushed the windows on windy nights, the trees and their sounds standing as borders of the mind itself.

She didn't forget to ask what lies outside; it never occurred to her to ask. The rules never occurred. She alone occurred, and he, and the house, and the clearing. What was cleared? From what? What lay beyond? You see, in asking we are outside the story, outside her mind. She would have blinked at the questions, as in too bright sunlight, and gone silent.

You could define her, place her, get to her mind, as a child will place miniature children in a toy house; or giants will lean over the chimney in a fairy tale, malevolent, beneficient; but interested. Something going on here; something of interest to me as well.

1

A down at the heels house in a small clearing. Three rooms, four rooms, five. Whatever you say. She could have added a room by ruminating about it; or substracted one. But there were limits; she couldn't make the house disappear, or wish Adam out of the way, or herself evaporate into sunlight. This is no fairy tale. In that sense, necessity, rules, order. Didn't fruit ripen and fall? It is said so. Once she put out her hand and caught a perfect fruit in the act of falling. It was so delicate, so unexpected and right, that it set her lightly pondering all the day long. As it would you or me.

I see linoleum underfoot, an old fashioned front hall, a rickety door giving on a nondescript grassy front plot. A big bed upstairs, about which more later. A semi-tidy kitchen, meals fair to middling, generally vegetarian, at this hour or that. Easy, easy all the way. It was not a motto; don't formalize. There were rhythms that came and went, mellifluous, the world now loud, now soft.

Old plank floors upstairs. Nondescript furniture, just short of beautiful or expensive (what's that?).

No friends (what are friends?); no children in the house (don't say "not yet," no such word).

People feel free, you can fondle the old clapboards of the house, or lean one eye in at the front window. Be bigger than all, be a giant before the childlike (what's that?) beginning of things. If it helps.

You're not to think of her as idle, though I have no idea what she did all day. But what's the use in asking? It's outside the rules, outside the story, which is about a man, a woman, a house in a clearing.

Still, I can tell you something. She was taking things in. She was taking in all the things one comes upon, being childlike before there are any children, in a clearing, in perpetual summer.

The law of things, the form of things, the meanings, colorations, subtleties, glancings, and then the fibers, ca-

2

bles, junctures, that grasped, linked, led further; the whole weave of things, invitations, metaphors. Watch out, language is on the way.

There was a tree, brawny as an oak but fruit-bearing, in the front yard. He'd slung a rope over a lower bough that went out horizontal, like a strong human arm. Then he hung an old tire from the rope. So she swung there, like a bird on a hoop; and she knew in her lucent body, bones and flesh and all, first motion, then silent motion, then the counter swing of the bough, which was like a great arm cantilevered from the shoulder, taking and giving; and from that, the steadfastness of the tree, which yielded not a whit to her weight, but stood there, stayed there, obeyed there.

You may believe this or not, it is not even a minor miracle. No great thing. One day she swung gently within the tire, and the bough swung with her, but with greater reserve, withholding. She happened to glance up, in awe and joy for the overarching canopy, the fruits like luscious suns, the breathing leaves. She put out her hand, no one told her to do it, no one told her the right moment or the right arc of her body, or what would loosen and fall. But it all happened together, her hand yielded an inch or two in delight and surprise, as though a weight were placed on a spring, the lovely fruit was hers, in her hand, red upon white. She started and stared and drew it to herself, clouded its roseate perfection with her breath, drew it down her bosom. The ruddy mirror cleared. Something happened to her at that moment, I think. Everything that came to be known later, in cruder times (after much tragedy and gross miscalculation as well as the spoilage of vast numbers of children, rotting like fruit in rancid barrels) the word was "education."

Which meant, the world came to her, as gift. A lesson in the pure freedom with which the world, when the world is allowed to be itself, gives itself. She was still mindless, if one thinks of the way minds function now. Which is to say, she received the apple—as her due. Which indeed it was. So she negelected to be grateful. Grateful? For what? To whom? Gratitude flourishes when rascals own the world. And that came later. (Gratitude, an afterword.)

As the fruit fell, so later we are told, the world fell. The former according to a sweet logic of things, the latter a catastrophe whose measure exceeds all blood, all crime, all breaking of bones and lives and minds.

Was there no one's hand to intercept, when the world fell? Did no one arrest its falling? Did no hand sense, like an instrument (ping!) the exact place and time for the exactly right act—and reach out, and intercede? We know nothing of this, nothing in our experience allows us inference of such a saving act.

Yes, I find her attractive and moving—and pitiful. A Swiss milkmaid lost in a city square. I find her inexplicable; her mystery, the cloud of unknowing that keeps me at distance is simply the cloud that becalms and fogs her in. She has never seen her own face. She has never wept.

After they made love upstairs in the enormous bed, silly as a walking camel, they fell asleep. In the morning she would ask, or he, what did you dream? One morning she said, I dreamed we were one, fused like two candles. And when our flame went out, we were two again. While we were one, we moved like a Roman candle or a cartwheeling child (there were no children). Now we are two, you a man, I a woman. And I think we are only second best, an afterthought.

Correction; she never said such things. The sentence is too reflective, it arches back on itself. It is not her style, it sees itself. And she never did, until afterward.

I wonder where he was, what he was doing, on The Day. With respect to those two, who stand at the fountainhead,

4

who are the prime and beginning, we are something like the gigantic child who kneels clumsily at the front window of the doll house. His very breath can cloud the proceedings within, he can work havoc by inadvertence. Watch out, your elbow is an avalanche.

If we stay within the confines of the story, and set up the walls and dependent roof, strongly, to stand true, to interlock, to contain, then when one leaves the story he leaves the house. And yet there is nothing but the two and the house, and the clearing. We can listen, perhaps, imagine the sound of sawing wood or hammers. Or close our eyes and hear him communing with plants and animals. (There was no speech yet.) From one point of view, he had only to be gotten out of the way, wandering, appraising, planning. She is the one we must watch. Out in the yard, swinging to and fro in the old sun-rotted rain-mottled Goodyear Snow Grip. Gifted, retarded, naive, worldly wise, back, forth, higher, lower, ridiculous, touching, suspended, anchored, she loves me, she loves me not.

Here it comes. An old wire fence, half given over to decrepitude, crawled along twenty feet from the tree, parallel to the dirt road. Woods, clearing, house, woods again; and the road. And the fence that kept no one in and no one out; since there simply was no one, except those within. A fence, and silly fence parts, half gone in the hoof, rotted and dry in the knee, knotted in the head, dependent on the long grass for shaky uprightness. Within, familiarity neither bred contempt nor fed curiosity. Went on swinging in the tire, mind neither commenting on the perfect day, nor registering, nor comparing, nor touching tomorrow or yesterday. A very vixen of content. A bovine mother of all.

Then at the gate (there was a non-gate, as there was a non-fence) there materialized—someone. He was there too suddenly (that was known afterward) to be her eyes' idle creation. Lounged there, hung there from the decrepit fence. A stogie in his mouth, a sack on his back. Mopping his brow. A figure perilously near a nobody, the first hobo maybe (not yet). Saying; bibles, ma'am. I sell bibles.

The woman was kind. A drink of water?

So he ambled forward. She had a few moments to take him in as he came toward the porch. The second of his kind, he would have been a visual bore. But he was the first.

And she was—not exactly bored (no sense yet) she was a touch weary (go slow now) of a world in which there was only herself, him, the house, the clearing; and for replicas, for others—only two shadows.

He came in. For five seconds, for five steps, he was exciting, like the fruit that fell, only darker.

Ten steps forward, two dirty shoes on the porch, he was a bore. Five sentences, he was a bore. It's a point worth pressing home. He had to push his wares to keep any attention at all.

He was so unlike herself, he was so unlike Adam, he should have been a perfect hit, a New Model coming in like that from nowhere, the first new voice, the only other in the world. Yet he aroused in her only an utterly wicked irresistible flex—a yawn. He made a warm day humid. He made kindly thoughts cloudy.

Imagine a game, a solitary game in the yard. She concocts a figure out of mud and straw, wraps it in old rags, sets it flat on its feet. Will it not have a mind of rotten straw, a thick speech, clayey? He did.

At first, at the gate, he had looked like nothing so much as a caterpiller on its haunches, oversize, sick green. She had to pretend respect (not knowing how to pretend). She didn't know yet, how different he was. In anatomy how singular, in mind what a peril. How could she know? The complaint is set down here, explaining what happened afterward. It would be magnified, like a cyclone, which at center eye is less than one inch in diameter, yet can suck the world to ruin. Daughters of Niobe, daughters of Jerusalem, your hour nears.

In anatomy; his crotch smooth and rubicund, a shaved peach.

No arse hole worth speaking of, cold there. He left these things out when he put himself together out of straw and clay, a poor third in the world. Let's raise us some hell, was all he thought; balls, bunghole, they were flim flam in a goose's trousers, who wanted food, who needed love? He had hell in mind; he knew the bible.

Mouth too was a deceit, before he ever spoke. It was not for eating, it was for holding unlighted stogies in, by a lip, thereby inducing confidence in the clientele, and betrayal. As for speech, also deceitful; bibles, ma'am. And that mopping of face. The truth was, he didn't sweat anywhere. He was wiping dust from his eyeballs, which were stone cold, tearless. Dust from his nose which was breathless as the grave.

Could she have known!

We're outside, speaking of inside; or after, speaking of before. And this was the danger; the sardonic half smile that half ate his face, together with those eyes lit in hell. He had one foot in after, one in before, cloven soul, schizoid. And double the might of knowledge to press down on her appalling innocence. Two hooves on her breast. It was so easy to bring the world down; a twitch of the bough, the fruit was his.

What did he know that she didn't know? Simply, everything we know; consequences. Not a threat or a curse or a sentence to be passed, but our world. Which is the bitter opposite of her world, and at least within the compass of the story (which is the compass of the possible, the not necessary, the once real) the real world.

7

We cannot imagine that world, let alone desire it. We can only despise it, and secretly mourn. She held the door open. He hitched himself up fusty, foolish, deadly, a goat playing god. And stalked in.

The Prison Letters of Cain

Dear Mom,

To let you know I've arrived. They brought in a busload of us last night. I'm tired as a dog. A long ride in the rain, all of us chained together, no stops for food. This is redneck country, we're supposed to yelp like dogs when they crack the whip.

One respect, I see what they mean, dog tired. I'll write later. You stay cool.

Cain

Dear Mother,

Pretty well settled. They have us high security types all splayed out in the joint, I never get to see the dudes I came down with.

I was sick as could be for 3 or 4 days, injections. You cross all those state lines by federal bus, they get ideas, what you might pick up on the way. What I picked up, a big flaming case of—loneliness.

Life ahead. Too long to think of. Hope you think of me.

Cain

Ambie,

Wanted to get a note off, time so slow, distances long.
I'm here, you're there. I hope school's not a drag. It
always was for me, part of it religion, religion, all those
freaky people putting us through our paces.

You're too young to remember Eden Mississippi.
What a laugh—if you had a mouth to laugh through
when they got done with you. We were on two
standards—gold and shit. A two-school deal, ours and
the real one. I used to wonder how they beat those nuns
in shape and divided them up, the crazys for us, the
brights for the whites. I used to imagine a shapeup hall
every morning, mother superior going down the middle
pointing over her shoulder: you there, you here.

It was awful. What do they think of me now? There
must be a lot of clicking molars and shaking heads.

You stand firm buddy. See you.

Cain

Dear Mother,

Some of these notes 'll get to you, some of 'em won't.
I'm trying this one by a friend. To tell you they've got
me in what these nazis call an "adjustment center."
Another friend got to my medico file. Appears I'm a
"compulsive schizoid." In other words, crazy as hell.

Result, they're drugging me up like mad. I'm
wandering around most of the day like a veg on wheels.

You get a lawyer down here right off, before I really
spin out. These assholes are crazy—really crazy. Shrink
told me with a slimy smile yesterday, I was responding
favorable. Favorable! If my soul was my arm, he had a
blade in his fat guts.

Cain

10

Mother,

Things are letting up. I got the books you sent. They held them up 10 days, fumigating them I guess. Settling down now. Hard to believe, 18 months gone by already.

How you feeling? I'm fine. Should have said sooner, it's so good that you write. When you came to see me once, I was lit up for days. I'm slow telling you how much it means. I'm here like an animal in a trap—not just my leg or big toe, but all of me—all my future, all my body and soul. And will be. A has-been from the start.

But when you cross the whole state of Ohio by night bus to spend a few hours in this stinking hole, and look so worn and then have to drag home again; it gets to my heart. I don't want to bug you with loose talk, a lot of living can't be undone. But I'm trying.

Cay

Mother,

Hey, that was a helluva letter you dropped on me. How come, just when I was trying to play things decent for a change? What the hell is it all about? Do you know what 24 hour lockup means, how my fingers tremble in the dark when they throw a letter in here at me? How I press it against the bars to catch enough light to read by? And then your downer! Ingratitude you say, all you did for us, all your broken dreams. BS lady!

Which being translated says, who wanted to be born anyway? And did I come popping out with some IOU tucked in my crotch, that you have to keep pushing at me through the bars? Ever hear the one about no blood from a stone? Squeeze me lady, dry bones, dry bones.

11

Sure things ended bad. Sure *his* blood is on me. I'm
here ain't I? Where do you want me, dead too?

Look, every hour of every stinking day you, God, and
that other silent old man you live with (and who never
gives me a single sign I exist) have your back payments.
Put out your hand lady my sweat will fall on it. Put it
out again, here's my crying. Want my blood, they'll
shortly arrange to send it on.

I haven't forgotten. But why don't you? Then I could
bear remembering. Don't write if you have to that way.

I will sign off. I remain your murdering son, paying
up dear.

K.

Ambie,

It's good to hear from you, what passes for living
outside. Picture me boy—an iron shoe box, beaten by
iron hammers, night and day. In between the beatings
I've got to think, eat, shit, walk, breathe, keep my heart
massaged.

There's a lot of blood around, not all of it in bodies.
Sometimes, a quick shove or a bullet, it gets to running
down skulls or bellies; that's the finish line. Other times
someone gets nicked in arm or leg or scalp—he lives to
have it mopped up—mostly by himself.

You know, I see life mostly through a bloody blur.
It's the only thing that binds the outside to the inside.
When someone falls over, either onto someone else or
onto cold earth, permanent, I know why I'm here. I also
know I'm going to be here, permanent mailing address,
so to speak, a grave. Deeper than a grave is my
knowledge, the deeper it goes, the more I dig. Unless I
keep head and armpits above the pit.

Question: What do you have left when you have

nothing left? I'll work on that one, you do too, let me
know.

But I was talking about blood. When I see it
streaming out do you know it talks to me? How's that
for a crazy head? But it does. If you're good, I'll tell
you someday what it says to me; and what I say back.
You've got to talk back, or you'll drown in it.

They're coming around with what passes, in the big
house manual, for a meal. No details, you wouldn't eat
for days.

I'll tell you this though, I dreamed of him last night.
Does that mean something's on its way? You don't tell a
thing, hear? Forget I talked to you, too.

Cain

Brother,

It's a week later, the blood has cooled, or been wiped
off, or like a snake, found another place to crawl into.
Anyway, it's gone.

But for me, it's never gone far. That snake's found
something to eat: me. Blood will have blood.

Especially (as I was telling in my last immortal line to
you) around here. Do you know this place is built of
dead bones plus the blood of the living? Old silence
used to tell us as boys how they built castles in Ireland
with field rock, bull's blood for a mortar mix. That's this
place; it stands and shall fall not. Nothing stronger than
the blood of the guilty, nothing harder than stones when
heads beat their pulp out against them. I should know.

Ten years ago I killed him. Knocking around this
circle of hell, the System, ever since. Ten years to die
over and over again, too dumb to die, too stupid to stay
down. I'm reading some good things: Guevera, Jackson,
Malcolm, Mao. They're saving whatever in me can still

13

go anywhere, which given the time and place, sure as
hell isn't my feet.

How's school, how's life, how's mom, how's that old
Attic Man?

I don't (strangely let it seem) have much advice for
you, though you're—how much?—ten years younger.
Sure you should have an older brother around. I wasn't
much of one, I'd be a fool to try to send you a package
deal for the good life. From here? That'd be a hot ice
cream from hell!

Sometimes though, when the madhouse wears out its
lungs and stops mid-beat for a sob, for a smoke, for a
death—my heart goes out to you. It leaves me choking.
Homesick, eating my gall, wanting to undo what can't
be undone, wanting that snake to turn into blood and
the blood to go back to his heart. And me and him to
be—brothers again.

Short of that (which is short of everything)—what?
My fist closes on—nothing. I watch my fist, open and
close. I see blood. My life, har har, I call it. Nothing, it
eats me alive. Nothing eating nothing. Want a taste?

Brother

Mom,

It's raining outside, the way I have it figured out on
my wall, it must be the first day of spring. I know, but I
can't tell you how. Something, pollen in the air, a breath
that's not a whiff of hell—it gets in, even here. And you
know—I go around like a drunk, though they've frosted
over the windows and what they haven't blacked out the
bird shit has. Never mind, spring. Makes my feet go like
those crazy springs we used to strap on and hop around
on, making your ankles go snap.

14

Do you know I dreamed of you all last night? Were we ever any different? Don't I have a right to ask?

I remember the look you used to have in your eyes, a summer evening, the softer light made even that dumb crude flat we lived in beautiful. Do you know how beautiful you were? Do you know what that look says, still says, across the years and bars and—murder? It says we were different. It says we crossed a line. It says you knew it, maybe you crossed it. It was something about new knowledge, big chunks, coming too fast to be swallowed, so they stuck in your throat. It was the look of someone choking, your eyes were red, there were sudden tears, you brushed them away and put your foot down sudden where you sat. As though it shouldn't happen, shouldn't be coming so fast. What shouldn't?

I want to say it; I think you knew, all along, something terrible was going to happen. I think you felt it a hand on your shoulder, only the hand was bone, your shoulder was bit by lye. Ate up the flesh. What did you know? I guess I'm asking because of that dream. Why do I, sudden as snap your finger, start dreaming—and of him? Christ, he lies low there, six feet under. Ashes to ashes. Who let him up again, that pipsqueek, that forever kid?

Let me tell you this, he was there last night (you tell old Stolid too, if he ever puts down his beer can for a minute) he was around here, trailing his bloody rags, looking in at me. How did I know it was him? How does one ever know, how could it be anyone else in the bloody world?

Like if in a slaughter house something else than beef or mutton hung there on the hooks moving, wouldn't you know? I'm an expert in beef and mutton, it's all around me, stamped low grade by the United States

15

meat combine. Don't I know something else if I see it, dead meat even, but human? I tell you he was almost human.

He came around here, he knew who I was, too. You can believe it. He looked through those black bandages. I could smell I was smelling him, a smelly dream not normally had by yours truly or anybody else. The bandage open for eyes, closed where the mouth was. And a hand, bone and nothing more, coming out of somewhere touching me, on the shoulder. Shoulder like yours, when lye touched you. What did it mean, what was he trying to say? I'll have to think about that a long time. You will too.

Your son.

Brother Ambie,

More than a week since I wrote mom a freaky letter all about a dream. Tell her please forget it. It don't signify—anything. If she was in here, she'd have nightmares too.

I'm going to classes, learning something about TV sets and car parts. That's really playing deaf, dumb and blind—so I can go on with everything that counts, from pushups to Che and Fanon. Don't forget, write something about what's happening at school, how ma is, what the old man is up to (say, for six and a half years besides beer and silence). Is he going to die that way, how does he think I feel? As him who's dead anyway. Ask him to try living for a change.

Yr Bro.

P. S. Anyway I'm sending on some notes I made the same day I wrote mom. You can read them or burn them or wipe yr arse with em, take your pick. But they

16

go with that freaky letter. Who knows, something crazy for the family record (ha ha).

(Notes—for Ambie and Ma only, for Pa if he wants.)

He came at me, my brother, black as a stove's belly. I knew him all right. I had a terror you don't know nothing about on two counts: 1) no one did him in but me, and 2) no one's here in consequence but me. Terror strikes out terror, so to speak. What did he look like? I don't know. I'd have to go back there eleven years to find out, and there's no way back. Who knows it?

He was there, I was dreaming. I confess through my finger writing this, my puny soul, he was there. And didn't say a word I can bring up to write down. Yet said it all.

I'm telling you everything. Being there, bony as a lightning fork, alight, moving and not moving. Moving toward me, putting that thing like a hand on my shoulder. And I, too dumb to shrink away; taking the lye to the bone.

It was worse than murder. I've done that. It was worse than murder or revenge after murder. I've escaped that, barely. Do you know what it was? What was worse than all of it put together? Forgiveness.

(4 days later)

The more I think of it. You see I know what the others do with their hands, their fists, judges, fuzz, even the Old Patriot in the old days. When they want you they grab you, they come down on you like a wall, their hand tightens like the trap of hell. This was something else. It was more like—mom's hand, when you were a sick kid in bed, half in half out of it, and yet you knew it was her hand, it could only be hers, it could only mean one thing. I love you.

I've cooled things four days now. I didn't want to put

down some dream crap I'd be laughing at years ahead.
Believe me I've done everything I knew to crate my
head. Even thought of shoving it in the toilet bowl,
good and cold. But its true its true, I can put my right
hand to left shoulder right where he gripped me. I can
feel it hot, cold, to the bone.

What it meant was, no more fooling around, he was
like a buzzard with a human eye, he was after me, that
grip was his message. Get it? I forgive you. You're my
brother. It was like the grip of God, bone to bone.

Will he come back? He was like death, if death had
hands. Brother brother, forgive me.

Dear Mom,

Marking eight years here today on the wall. They
supply a wall so you can mark your life on, tic tac toe.
I'm sorry as hell to learn old Thunderjug is ailing.
Please tell him, if he finds the mention of my name
mentionable, I'm ailing too. I call the disease Life In the
Iron Shoe Box. Tell him I don't wish when I wish the
worst to anyone in sight, that the father spend one lousy
hour where I've spent years and years. Tell him if you
want to, the old dream of brother keeps coming back,
same zombie, same message. Ask him why we have to
wait for the dead to forgive the living. Tell him. What
the hell. Tell him to go to hell or something.

Your Son.

P.S. What's the opposite of my birthday? That's what
this is. Blood in your eye.

Dear Brother,

You know why I'm writing this, mom wrote the old

18

man's worse. I want a few things on the record so he can read them, or you can read them to him, or tell him, or something. You do it.

Life still goes on, I won't waste time saying its only bearable because it's here, it's always been here. It'll always be. I'm here. So be it.

What I want him to know, sometime before he dies, is that dream. Because he's in it. He shouldn't die easy without hearing about it. What's he so quiet about anyway? He isn't dead yet. I'm the dead one, tell him that. Tell him about that dream, you hear? What it's about is what it's always been about. Murder. And in consequence. Where I find myself, where we all find ourselves, why ma cries so much. It isn't being poor, it isn't me being here. It isn't her being sick so much. It's the dead. You should know that, I should know that. We all have to. Otherwise all this is saying nothing, standing up, a big laughing stock. All the big numbers I'm constantly having laid to me isn't a lb. of fly shit. Tell him. You tell him that. How brother keeps coming back. How he'll keep coming, till we all die, or change, or accept. I don't know how to put it, do the best you can.

Am I getting you the message, that only the dead understand the dead? That's what I'm saying. I'm dead, sure as he is. And I don't care, anymore than he does.

Bone meets bone. That's how he comes. He doesn't even have to leave the dead to find me. I'm there. We're cell mates. You know when a brother puts his hand on you. You know it. Nobody has to tell you. Well that's me. Now you tell the old man what I've set down here. Tell him to forgive me. Tell him the dead want the living to forgive. Tell him I'm forgiven—by everyone but my father—and how come. You can tell mom too, but there's more time for that. What I want him to know is all I've said to you. And you put your hand on him when you say it. You hear? Dammit, you write me back you hear, and did it.

Loving you Brother, Cano

How Noah
Missed the Boat

But how could he hate what he had made?

The question is naive as hell, young man. He didn't hate what he had made, he hated what they had done with what he had made. There's a difference, you know. Quite a difference.

If I thought the answer smelled a little of rote and prior instruction, this wasn't the time to say so. I was sitting at the bedside of the only genuine savior the world had ever known; the one who had saved a few mortals (including himself) while jettisoning just about everyone, and everything, else.

Now he was dying.

What he had gained for himself was not easily said. A statue in a park, a name in the books. And some time, undoubtedly, not much time but a little.

Now that little was running out, too. He lay there like a stone. Eyes closed. Breath blowing his little pursed lips in and out. Noah dying; the savior unseamed. Hands drumming away, spastic, a lost tune. Blue as thin milk, immersed in blue water, clinging to some scrap of debris, keeping afloat awhile longer.

He opened his eyes.

What did I gain? I'll soon know, won't I? Or what I lost. Or something of both.

I had a choice, you know. I was one of the first, who had

21

any choice worth a spit. Not one of the others, over the whole blasted round of the world, had any choice. So they did what they did. And it stank in the nostrils—and not only God's.

Choice? Their only choice was what place to take in the infinite procession of fools. How to be fools. How to surpass other fools. How to act it out. How to glory in it. Colors, styles, fabrics. One could dress in a thousand absurd ways, all of them befitting the time. Irresponsible, conniving, cruel, quaking with lust—there was a style to fit. There was a public to applaud. Oh no! No lack of a public. It was their blind substitute for a community.

They all went one way, huckstering, buying, selling. And the outcome no one knew or cared. Choice! Someone else was choosing for them. The whole world was governed from below. There were gears and shafts and pulleys chugging away underground. And they danced along, or were dragged along, the appointed track. And called it freedom. Freedom! They would have shriveled under its least breath.

What they were absolute masters of, experts in, was slavery. Round and round and round they went. They proved it pretty early you know, the whole planet was a closed system, round as a shaved head, round as the ball welded to a chain—welded to every one of them.

Freedom! They were created for it, of course. That's how they left the starting gate. But not one of them had ever tasted it, or wanted to.

Do you know what that meant to Him? To see his handiwork warped, rotted out of all recognition?

It was an atmosphere, like a belt around the earth; a filthy girdle; nothing could be seen for what it was. Your eyes would smart and redden, just living in it. And it kept tightening. The whole pattern and form of things going slack. Freedom, love, hope, that look on faces that carry some dignity—going somewhere, creating, moving toward life.

Gift, achievement—what could those things mean among such people? Nothing! Nothing He could recognize, as his own, as their own. Smirking marionettes, whores, pimps, sellouts, killers, living by the buck, dying for the buck, murdering for the buck. You can't imagine it, today.

God used to hold his nose, coming among them. He'd be blind for days after. Blind with rage, blind in his head. It was smog from the dump they were treading, the city dump they had made of the sweet earth. Hell was pumping the bellows.

How could it go on, he said to me one day. (He was quite calm. He'd kept away from them for a week to think things over.)

We've a crisis on our hands, he said. When I imagined all this, when I put it together, I had a few bad hours, thinking of where it might all go. But this! He put his hand across his eyes, palm out. I'd never seen him like that before. It was enough to turn your heart over.

He sat there, eyes cold as death, all his fires banked. He looked at me, reading my heart like a surgeon, thinking things out, ways out, double intent, jeopardy, seven good reasons for not undertaking this eminently just war. No go. No go, as I could see. More time! A phrase. More time for what? More time for murder. More time for duplicity, greed, hatred, money getting, blood letting. Everything that went under the heading, creative leisure in the good society. I was pleading for his yes, my own heart was saying no.

As was his. You see, we read one another like a book. He could draw the veil at times, a little jealous, even petulant, when he got a feeling I was reaching too far, too deep into his heart. He didn't know it, that was a way of giving himself away too; I could read even his silence.

To speak of the two of us; it's germane to the whole case. We were like two mirrors set opposite, one face front and

23

back, like two facing books, open, literate, two mouths
signaling, two eyes opposite two eyes. A thousand years, a
single day. I was too recently out of his hands to forget their
press, their import. Nor could he forget the subtle grit and
smear of my clay, its smell even; the moment when under
his breath, I warmed into flesh and bone. He was like a
mother. I was his son, son enough to speak up on occasion.
He liked that, even while he hated it, bridled under it.

But what could he do? Find a better son? I tell you the
world was a disgrace that cried aloud for vengeance. He
went among them—and they mocked him, made sport of
him. He was treated like the village fool on market day. The
world was drunk, half off its feet; he walked among them,
the one who would neither pipe nor dance their tune.

He went into their midst, again, and again. He was patient all right. You can't realize it, living after the catastrophe. He tried for maybe—a hundred years or so. First every
day, then every week or so, then finally, draggingly, unhap-
pily, hardly at all. Toward the end, they were so blind, they
were raging through the world like mad dogs, mouth to
tail, tail in mouth, faster and faster, a fool's dance, a death
dance. They were people turning into animals, animals
turning into slime.

You have to see him in the middle of this mad ring,
closed, whirling on itself. He was a pillar of salt, weeping,
bitter, tasting his own bitterness. But he was stern, too. And
growing, growing in resolve, salt purifying itself, keeping
its savor against the stain and filth their hooves were kicking
up.

I saw it; he was being torn apart. It wasn't just that they
were self destructing, nothing so simple. It was a new presence in things. An emanation. Someone else had taken the
reins of the world. There was an adulterer in the sweet
marriage bed. He'd crawled in there, snickering to himself.

And worse. From horrified screams and shrinking away

—the bride had come to terms. Adjusted as they say. When she met God, after one of her episodes, she offered him silence, sweet smiles, a cover up. And he knew the truth, all the while. The bride was whoring it—with a stench, a plague, a leer, a fang, a hoof. She was bedding down with a beast, a beast inside the world's body, sowing death there. You had only to look around, the day's conduct followed the night's, to the letter.

A hundred years of it. He gave in slowly. He was so slow, a dunce, to believe evil of people. Patience was his greatest weakness, maybe the only one. Patience, he'd say over and over, while we looked at each other deaf and dumb and blind.

He said patience. It was what the bridegroom chewed on, a bitter root. Patience; and all the while he was being conned, cuckolded, lied to, derided. It took forty days to wash it all away, over the edge, forever. Today people hear of it and are appalled. They won't quite say it; only in their hearts. How impatient he must have been!

They don't know what he went through—someone else in charge of the world. That's what couldn't be borne. That was what stuck in you. What couldn't be healed, covered over. Someone else in charge, every day, setting the gears in motion, opening him, piping the tune of the universe, ordering the dance underway.

So he pulled the chain.

The old man leaned back, pale as the sheets he lay on, drained. Lay there, skinny as a fence post, but alert, on edge. Ready to take me on again, the Great Survivor. Glorying in his respite, death evaded and death nearing. Don't they all want to talk, talk, talk at the end?

I'd give him talk. I wanted to shake him till he rattled, serene bag of bones, patriarch, conniver; grinning or sober his look said, don't lean on me boy, I've got perpetual immunity.

25

Like hell you have. I've listened like a doorpost. Now it's your turn; old man. Who was it gave you the franchise, this "access to the divine"?

Who struck that bargain? Wasn't your being snatched from the flood, the price of being lost—to humanity, to yourself?

And rolling it all into one, how do you qualify as "father of a new race, of new men and women," when you started out with a bargain that wipes out everyone but yourself? Didn't everyone else die because you washed your hands of them—in the flood?

He came back quick. It's you who's coming down like a flood. But I'll take you on. I've taken on tougher ones than you.

First of all, of course, I was one of them. Who ever denied it? I was born of their tribe, my sons and daughters came of them. But still. I was not one of them. I'll say it with my last breath. I was not. I was on the other side. I wasn't about to run with a herd—a herd that was turning into a pack. Oh we had friends here and there, but in the end, they ran with the others, too. And we were alone.

Do you have any idea what that means? I bet you don't. I'll tell you. I had to gather up everything, take it all, children, wives, herds, into the wilderness. Flee for our lives, for our souls. That's where your question falls flat. It wasn't a matter of quietly choosing God and letting everything else go. Not so simple! I wanted to be faithful to the whole thing—God, the others. That was my pull, my anguish. If I manuevered it all into something simple—"God without the people"—why, he would have stopped the show, ordered us back to the tumult and frenzy and crowds and sin, dumped us there; make the best of it. No he kept us in the struggle, closed the door on us, kept us trying. He kept us in the pit—as long as his own patience . . .

I had all I needed out of him, at least all I could reasonably expect. I got out of there, I wanted no more of him weighing on my mind.

Had he answered anything, justified anything? Only the direct line survived, of course. Only his line. Which is, of course, our line, too. Which may have accounted for the side long glint in the old man's eye. Don't get high and mighty; you're in this, too. The taint, so to speak, in the eye of the beholder.

Still, everything granted, questions remain. Could he have cared for anyone outside his clan, since he (and his god) had drawn the line so hard and fast? With the expectation, of course, that the flood would wash away the evidence of any line at all. Just as it washed away those who (by sublime decision of His Impenetrability) stood outside. Everything washed away. No line, no corpus delecti. Therefore, no motive.

Crime? Whose crime?

Well, the debate isn't over. Not if eternity makes any sense. And just in case, here are a few questions for the old man, whatever shore he's beached on. Questions, I believe, that lie outside the competence of any earthly court.

Noah, who were your friends in those "days of sin"? Tell us about them.

Isn't the death dance a rather restricted circle from which to judge the world?

Were there none besides your virtuous selves who refused to take part in the dance, or who took part reluctantly, who were perhaps longing for some other way?

(There being, as you know, too, nothing more deadly monotonous than killing others or putting them down or, on the other hand, dancing to another's tune.)

And what of the children?

And what of the old people?

Is it inevitably the "highest types" who climb aboard the S.S. Salvation when the skies begin to fall?

Who paid for your trip, and in what coin?

Did your god give up on everyone because he was tired of playing the village fool? Name for me, please, a better role for your god.

If you, Noah, are the saving remnant, who are you saving now? Where's your life at, in the inelegant phrase of the young? And your wives? Are they liberated? And your children, are they better (what's a better child?) than the others, the ones who slid under the waves?

Who's this god anyway, that by his decree some die and some live? We never quite got his criterion clear.

In fact, since he purportedly made us, what's wrong with his hearing about who made him? Does he think he could survive, without us—even without our foolishness and revolt?

What does he do on his days off?

Try this one; I think his despair with us is premature. After all, we haven't despaired of him.

Maybe you were too much in his corner to be able to offer an argument for survival. Survival of everyone, that is.

When you dined on the town, who paid the bill? What do you make of this statement, set down in possible self-interest: "even fools deserve to survive"?

And of this: I never saw anyone improved by death. Did those who perished get improved? In what respect? Show us; otherwise the lesson is, to say the least, incomplete.

What became of everyone after they drowned? Where are they now? Some of us would like to know; call it self-interest again.

Did you, or he, ever hear of Jesus? Do you think Jesus' treatment of people is somewhat different than yours? If so, which god should change methods? And (with this I close) will he please come around someday (as you say he did for quite a while in your day) in our simpler times of more direct and wicked fun, days that make yours look like a picnic in the nursery—will he come around please, and crouch under our brimstone umbrella? And walk the streets among our gun totin' cits, when the clothing of practically every human on earth conceals a lethal charge? Also will he sniff the streams we can't swim in or drink from? Also, will he stay reasonably honest amid such duplicity as would make Satan a registrant in the local day-care-pre-school for toddling liars? And having tried a few of these things including, of course, the effort required to breathe with a tightened noose around his neck, would you or he please tell us (we never heard) the real meaning of that rainbow he once made much of?

And with this, dear old remnant of a savior, as promised above, I close, wishing you the best. Namely, that your spirit may transmogrify into that bird that once floated along unconcerned and undrenched as you please above the waters.

And if by chance or prescience you do (it does), please come back to us bearing that bit of green which, though none of us has seen, none of us can quite forget.

Come with the widest smile and the brightest eye you can summon out of your improved status. For we don't need saviors so much as we need signs. And perhaps in one way or another hinted at above, you and he owe us something along these lines, no?

The Tower
of Brotherly
Love Blah, Blah

Our scene is the city of Brotherly Love. In this city, everyone once used the same language, that of Brotherly Love. No one can say exactly in what this tongue consisted, since (as we shall see) the Language of B. L. is now a lost tongue. In any case, the brothers once said one to another, let us build ourselves a tower with its top in the heavens. Now this tower was to be built according to the ethos of Brotherly Love, that is to say, monetary considerations were all but laid aside, whatever commerce was transacted in the tower was done in the spirit referred to above, there was to be no fooling around, chicanery, double dealing, misappropriations. Nothing of the sort. Such things be far from us, the brothers said, holding hands around a big table during a prayer breakfast; far north as New York, far south as Washington, D.C.; but here, never. So the tower went up, a marvel known as Zuggerat, only built in the modern manner, with stanchions of forged steel and windows looking out on every point. Let us make a name for ourselves, the brothers said to one another. Let's do this thing up brown.

So it was done. The tower arose and arose and arose, in such wise that the typographical arrangement of this page, down and down and down, seems a curiously wrong way to tell the story of the tower.

But let us see.

After some months, the Lord came down from heaven to view the tower which men had built. He was not pleased. He said, "Truly, these Brotherly Love people are all united, and speak the same language. This is only the beginning of what they will do. Hereafter they will not be restrained in anything they determine on." Then the Lord in a fit of chagrin stamped his left foot on the northwest corner of the top story of the splendid Zuggerat. The building shuddered slightly, people within paused in mid-motion, almost in mid-heartbeat. Coffee cups rattled in their saucers, papers floated off desks airborne, expensive cigars dropped their ash ppfffft! on raw silk suits. Then someone laughed shakily and said, a sonic boom somewhere. And Brotherly Love and its loving commerce resumed. Weeks went by, weeks of loving and exciting commerce all over the building. The brethren bought and sold, traded and swapped, breakfasted and prayed, and made money as before. Then quite suddenly something went wrong. Fine and intemperate as crows feet in a baby's eyes or cobweb defiling a holy place, a tracery of cracks began to appear in the northwest walls of the tower. They came in the summer, quiet and wrong as hoar frost. When they were patched up, they came back, quieter and bigger than ever. It was uncanny; like a stain, like a hidden crime in the walls, like the cry of a dead mouth. They were patched, the cracks came back worse than ever, the ungrateful dead. Everyone saw the thing, it couldn't help being seen. And everyone, especially those who knew that not all commerce in the building was brotherly and loving, kept mum. No one saw anything, no one knew anything. The word passed from top echelon to bottom; keep mum. What cracks in the building, they answered all comers indignantly. Those aren't cracks, they're cobwebs. The cleaning crews are goofing off again. It's being seen to.

The cleaning ladies noticed it; things kept getting worse. Mop pails wouldn't stay put. You'd turn your back, mop in hand, and the creepy pail would follow you across the room like a child's toy on wheels drawn by a child. Only there wasn't any toy, just a pail on wheels, sloshing quietly to itself, going its own way. Or you'd turn your back and the pail would creep into a corner like it needed to relieve itself. This way or that it went of its own sweet will, never where you left it. Unsettling as hell.

First by night and then by day, things got worse in the tower. People would line up to get on the elevator in the morning, people famous and lowly, sweet faced, blank eyed, underpaid secretaries motivated to their plucked eyebrows, corn fed horse traders chomping at the bit, another day to praise the Lord and pass the buck. They'd all get in the elevator, eyes on the lighted numbers of their proper floor; the elevator light blinking like God's eye in a Masonic window indicating the only possible American brotherly loving direction: UP. Invariably the car went UP, purring furrily in its track like a mortician's Cadillac. One morning things started like all the other mornings. Only, as the UP car slowed to its first stop, it gave a slight lurch, a tremor, hardly noticeable, but there. One tremor, then another, the car traveled on up, ever so slightly off balance, then on like a practiced drunk. It went up, but there was a rumble in its guts. At floor ten, the doors unlatched like two jaws, with a snarl. Good God, it seems to be going sideways, one typist said to another as they stepped out unsteadily. She was pale under her roseate pancake. Her companion, green around the nostrils, nodded. Their day was off to an unwanted bad start. The upstart elevator continued UP, at its own sweet pace, an unsteady jog, two steps UP, one step aside.

Things got worse. The passengers held their breath and prayed. UP or DOWN, it was like being stuck in church, under the eye of God, during an earth tremor. You hoped for the best and hung on, you had nowhere to go.

By night the repair crews came in; they sweated and climbed around the cables and tinkered and swore. We can't guarantee you anything, the boss told the tower super, the whole building's off its rocker. You ordered the wrong damn machine for this place. Elevator, hell; what you wanted was a cable car. He leaned forward, he snickered unpleasantly. I'll

tell you what this place is doing, it's sinking.
And it's sinking left foot first. You got troubles
buddy.

The rumors grew, thick as bats in a dead bel-
fry. The *Inquirer* phoned, CBS began to snoop
around. But the brothers were ready, the word
came down, cool it, stonewall it. Kickbacks?
Bribes? Laundered money? Deals? 'The idea
was downright outrageous, don't be an ass,
this is the Zuggerat of the City of Brotherly
Love, isn't it?

But when the Lord heard all this, he got really
angry. Putting up a lousy unsafe prefab was
one thing, but this mummery and mystifica-
tion! He thought and thought. Then he said,
snapping his fingers, "I've got it. Let's go
down and confuse their language so they will
not understand one another's speech." So he
ordered the tower surrounded at its top story
by 40 archangels, instructed in the following
manner. They were to float slowly down the
building with arms like a ring of Saturn, inton-
ing at every window and door, Mummery
Mummery Mystify, Mummery Mummery
Mystify. So it was done.

And all of a sudden, as though at a signal, CBS
rushed in at the front doors, 50 reporters with
pencils and pads, 20 TV teams, 45 radio inter-
viewers, enough to cover every one of the top
and middle grade executives of Brotherly
Love. Within five or six minutes, you could
hear and God could hear, and the angels could
hear, from every office and executive suite,
under cameras, into mikes, and onto scratch

pads, from worried mouths and cynical mouths and earnest brotherly loving mouths, only the following.
BabbleBabbleBabbleBabbleBabbleBabble Babble.
They couldn't get it together. One said, absolutely no one's fault, seismic tremors had developed under the building, how could it be anyone's fault? Another said, yes we're studying the remote, very remote possibility that someone not associated with our city or our Zuggerat, an out of state connection, set us up for this. Another read a statement: It is inconceivable that in this city such a loving and brotherly project, under the unassailable sway of ecumenical Masonic and B'nai Brith and Knight of Columbus brothers, should be sabotaged like this, goddamit.
No use. It was all over. And God smiled. And the F.B.I. moved in.
Now in conclusion let me revert to the typographical arrangement of this page (down and down and down) a method which is carefully chosen and in the opinion of the author, well fitted to symbolize the Tower. Let's listen to the prophet of the Lord, in this case a smiling rather untidy middle aged Swedish architect. As far as could be learned by exhaustive scrutiny of all sorts of files, he had no visible connection with brotherly interests. So he was brought in as advisor to the investigators of the sinister sinking tower. But you and I know who sent him. And he stood there in front of the cameras, and said with a straight face, Usual procedure in my country is to build a

tower from the foundation up; but America is
so rich, they reverse things. This tower was, by
every account, built from the top story down.
So was this story, built from the top down;
which may be the wrong way; or again, may be
the right way to tell of a wrong way. You
judge, but thank God also for his prophet, the
Swede. Not everyone is a babbler. We don't
have to be.

The Flea in Pharaoh's Ear

——Get ready for this one. I'm a flea in Pharaoh's ear. And I have a story to tell.

——I'm a rat in Pharaoh's palace. More about this.

——Flea: I must say at the outset, I'm delighted with my vocation. Learn to move around quietly, never disturbing a damask sleeve or a fold of skin. And then the things I hear, the things I could tell!

——Rat: Vile But Interesting; my biography. Survival, in a scene obsessed with grandeur and its meticulousities, becomes an art. I'm making it.

——Pharaoh (Flea speaking) has a mole on his groin. He also has piles. I know, I've been there. No one, of course, remotely imagines how careful I have to be. Rule one: travel by night. Start off by crooning a dream, something about conquest, mastery, adulation, in his ear. That gets him settled down. Then I start roaming, up and down the Supernal One, scalp to sole. Pharaoh owns Egypt but I own Pharaoh.

——This A.M. I, rat, went through his garbage. They do tend to be careless around the back door of the palace,

39

where he never ventures. Well, their excess is my redress, as the poor man knows.

He likes leeks, grasshoppers in wine, pheasants, oysters, strawberries, marinated small mushrooms, Nile herring. Lots of bread, lots of gravy, too much meat. Hardly an integrated diet. No wonder he doesn't even guess I'm around, his brain is sodden. And I'll bet he has piles.

This inspection tour, you understand, is no more than psychological reconnoitering. I wouldn't touch his menu with a stick—unless it was to change it to good golden Nile wheat, on which my family has thriven for a thousand years.

——Flea: I was reflecting only this morning, I shouldn't wonder if my activity hadn't given birth to that wonderfully inspired expression "to bug." In a double sense: 1) to use technology for overhearing, eavesdropping, etc., and 2) to annoy, to harrass. I do both, and love it. I hang like a scarab from the lobe of his ear, for hours, while he's sounding off; some of the most pretentious, labyrinthive talk ever heard on the planet. I cling there, eyes closed, ears open. Mostly smiling. Fascinating, the vagaries of power.

Yesterday here, tomorrow gone. They're on a different time scale; so they go in for sophisticated cruelties. A recompense, I suppose, for their sense of suffocation, the grave smell in their nostrils. Ah, these Big Ones, creatures of a day, an hour.

You should see his torture chambers. Women, children, old men—anyone that strikes up against his whims and obsessions. He grabs them, throttles them, freezes them, roasts them alive. Then they simply disappear.

But we don't. Someday, one or another of these royal scissorbills is going to put on his golden cheaters, look around, and find that under his very nose, here, there and everywhere, civilized communities are flourishing. Flea communes. The good life. Where rust and moth enter not.

And this one's blood is rotten; he's already begotten several near idiots. All this fuels his frenzy; he's got to make a mark, somehow. So he's building again.

——Rat: They build everything of stone. That doesn't allow much leg room for us. Still, there's that big sun boat he's so in love with, a transport to eternity. Beaten gold on the outside, panels of his exploits, cat gods, snake gods, sun gods. Infested with gods. I looked in vain for a rat god; nothing. And while it depresses me that he can see nothing of the divine in us, I reflect with considerable satisfaction—his ignorance is our survival. These fools can't even die without an orgy of killing. But there'll be no roundup of rats!

It's not clear to me as yet (I've only tried this for fifty-two years) why I keep choosing to be a rat. Item: I'll have to become more reflective, more self-critical.

——Flea: My own vocation gets clearer every day I hang around (!) Pharaoh. Last night I concocted the latest in a series of dreams that have sent him cold turkey. This morning he looks like a damp bed sheet. And Nefertiti's buttery concern at breakfast only succeeds in giving him the knip-shins. Another day, a good start.

He pushed away his plate and bellowed out a summons to his motley crew of magicians. They ran in, all aquiver, defeat in their dogs' eyes. He's already threatened several of them with the mines or the pyramids.

I can't blame them. He's a killer in this mood. Now hear ye! He gives out his latest dream, between clenched molars. He wants action, he shouts. Tell me what it means—sheaves, empty barns, sick cows!

The usual scene follows, a maelstrom. They don't know what to make of my images, I pile level on level. They stutter, smile sickly, put their heads together, lie like camel

41

drovers. Finally he curses them out of the room.

Off they go, bumping one another in the rear, sweating with relief. What a recessional!

He sits there all morning chewing his beard, red eyed with insomnia and terror. O Pharaoh, poor man, indeed, only a flea for friend!

———We rats have never been content with mere survival. Given the world, survival can be quite a feat. But the longer I hang around the world in this sack of bones, this revolting tail, these noisome appetites, the more I come to see things from a rodent point of view. To wit: find your niche, the world will fall in to your hands, ripe to the pick.

It's hard even to get under the Unholy Phony's shadow. Yesterday I tried, just for the fun of it. They were having some sort of religious procession; his train was a full twenty feet long, all peacock feathers and gold threads. I rolled into a ball, hid out in one of the folds. It pleased my sense of irony to hang on there, by my teeth; death amid glory.

Then a mishap; near curtains for Life Phase 182. They had paused at one of the big wayside sanctuaries, he was shouting redundant phrases into the breeze, everyone was grinning and bearing and bowing (self-praise is their wasting disease) when the wind whipped against his robe, nearly dumping me out of my cradle. Worse, a soldier caught sight of me; he would have darted forward to stomp me, but he didn't dare, for his very life; it's death to step out of line while Festerhead is doing his thing.

Nonetheless, I'd had enough for one afternoon. I transformed myself into Flea and appeared quietly on Big P's bejeweled ear lobe. There I stopped my ears against the auditory pollution, looked up to heaven, let it all go by.

———Flea: He's desperate. Last night I stung him on the bung with another dream. He started up like a blade on a spring, called for the lamps, and sat there biting his knuckles until dawn.

Why do I do it? I'll tell you.

I want him to misuse his power, which is to say, to use it normally. With normal ruthlessness, normal duplicity, a normally mounting ration of murder. I want him plunged deeper into the morass of his own ego. I want him—Pharaoh.

As I see things, I'm around simply to encourage him to develop his talents, insights—prepare his niche in the pantheon.

Dreams are of the essence, you see. He can't know himself without them. Good dreams like this: I run a coronation, a triumph for him—every night, if I please, tickling his ego into fits of ever more frantic laughter, frantic ambition. And bad dreams, of course. Turn him hot, turn him cold. I hold his head over the abyss like a vomiting child. I want him to taste the death at the heart of the world, at the heart of existence. To taste—what I taste. To know that death calls the shots, points the finger, brings down the sword on the bowed head. I want everything turned toward that baleful knowledge; religion, economics, imperial wars, slaves washing his feet, slaves breaking stones for his pyramids. I want him the slave of bad dreams. Then he'll proceed to verify them in life.

He thinks he serves the gods. I want him to think that. He thinks he's just, has just men around him. Let him think so. He thinks that being Pharaoh is an excellent way of being human. Yea verily. His council room is like an echo chamber; he loves to hear his voice bouncing back, then he knows he's an original. Original? He's about as original as sin. He breathes deep, inflates himself, like a bull frog with elephantiasis, points virtuously to the latest mitigation game; mitigation of injustice, mitigation of slave conditions, mitigation of torture. There, he bellows, aren't

I always improving things? The plebs now have, for the first time in history, an eighty hour work week, free beer on my birthday, free funerals. And yet they have the nerve to complain, demonstrate, strike. No sense of history, no idea how infinitely worse, how inhuman, things are in Phoenecia or Babylon. Why if they tried their didos on any other king, they'd be in boxes by sundown.

That's how I want him, old mitigator alligator. I've set his sights so low he can hardly crawl under them. Keep him mitigating, keep his grinders to the ground, keep his sights low, move them lower.

You see I have a job, too. Sometimes the smallest particle on the lowest scale of life has its place, its dignity, its vocation.

I'm a flea, but I'm a kingmaker, too. Don't tell him. I also break kings.

———Rat: I've never gone in much for doubts. We rats don't have that luxury, which presupposes honor, an aura, space, acceptance, a place on the web of life. But what do you do, when they hold their noses, scream, put their heels to your head, stomp you, drive you off the face of the earth?

Indeed, where can we go? They've declared war on us, total war, a war of generations, a war written into every birth, every marriage, every property deed. Every hand shake, every embrace—the assumption is there; rats are horrendous, lethal, spiritually disgusting, carriers of disease, necrophiliacs, robbers of graves!

When I think back on the lean centuries my people have endured. It's easily seen now; there was a wrong joint in the universe, that others should be so high and we so low. We cried out for a liberator, a hero, a visionary! Someone to reject, once for all, the herd view; that every rat is a pack rat, that we emulate those sweating hordes, building the imperial tombs under the lashes.

None of that any more. The best among us, our ideologues, those capable of grasping rat praxis, reject slavery even as we reject property. We travel light, we work at our own tasks.

No middle place. It came to this, we are radicals, or we are nothing. So we developed our formula, elaborated in a handbook composed by my lowly self. Like this: you're their problem; in consequence, they're your solution.

Not of course, that we didn't always have a history, a dignity. Else how could we go on—so far and so fast? Rats exist, as I see it (as the handbook puts it), to dramatize neglected aspects of the human psyche (insofar as humans may be said, by analogy with us, to possess anything resembling a soul). We are the voice from the outhouse. So to speak. Even the turds grow eloquent. Remember, man.

But enough of the past. One day, a momentous breakthrough. Meditating at my humble sewer door, I saw it; light at the end of the tunnel. Sick of hiding out, sick of running, sick of being their international universal loser. Where could a rat go?

What was it I might become, young and stalwart, superior IQ, good family background, languages, astrology, unafraid of hard work, disciplined, reasonably good falsetto, total recall. What could I become, for the sake of my people, to wipe out once and for all, our historical ignominy?

Connections. That was it.

Let's play around with that one. Who is it of all the world, by common assumption and everyday adulation, in the kingdom, in his ego, is furthest removed from the lowly estate of—rat?

Yes. Paraoh.

I had my connection. I would become Pharaoh's Rat-in-Residence.

May I say, in that resolve, at a single stroke, I had stolen fire? Indeed, from that day on, the destiny of our people was assured. When men got too complacent, overweening, we struck back. The ultimate weapon. Though Lucifer knows we use it with the greatest discretion, only after long and arduous persuasion, intimation, dramatic acts, only after all else has failed. Our wars are just wars.

I don't want to give too much away. But I am authorized to say—we're the ultimate Major Force. One great element of our power is, of course, persuading Pharaoh he's the ultimate force. We prop him up. Even I, in my humble present form, play his footstool, his cowering and cornered enemy.

In just such ways, which might be summed up as the Diplomacy of Disappearance, we guarantee two things. First Pharaoh, our cover, will live and die under the most stifling sublime self-convinced delusions of power.

And number two, we shall survive.

Black Death, anyone?

——I, flea, admit to being faintly disturbed.

As candor is of the essence of our method, I set this down, knowing that it shows us at something slightly below our best.

Pharaoh has slaves, of course, thousands of them. Never mind how many, he doesn't care; knowing their number is as useless to him as knowing the number of hairs on his scalp. He has slaves, leave it at that. Another way of saying he's Pharaoh.

For our part, we've learned a great distrust of slaves. They're—how to put it—an extreme instance of degradation under pressure. Like putrid juices in a heated vat, always on the verge of erupting.

From our point of view, this is not useful. We like socialized mediocrity; topped off by a tyrant, preferably toward the thin end of a blood line, compensating for his dumkopf with a flagrant ego. With such a one we can work. We dust off his gods, remolding their faces, so he's really looking in a mirror when he kneels to worship them. But I've gone into our method elsewhere.

Slaves! I hate them with a passion, those faceless, brainless, defiled brutes. Nothing to lose from birth, given to spasms of despair. They simply don't know their place! They learn one foolish word from the lexicon, hoist it on a pole, tear it to tatters; revolution!

They really want (I set this down in full cognizance of its absurdity, its unimaginable stupid pretention)—they want to emulate us.

They really believe, blockheads, that they can seize the reins of history—drivers, ha! Planners, leaders, the big boys.

N.B. Take more heed of what's going on in the work camps. Especially the Jewish ones.

More heed; someone called Moses.

And in the prison; someone called Joseph.

The Body Count
of King David

The sins of those in power can be summarized roughly as follows: what they want, they take.

This being the case, it is difficult, indeed, to discover an interesting sinner among the powerful.

Their sin is such a remarkably predictable phenomenon, one wonders if there is not some sort of crude Mafia Conduct Handbook passed along and along and along, as characters to the manor born succeed to the Orb. Take what you want, the liturgy of enthronement intones; take it, it's yours. Women, flocks, turf, warriors ("My men") servants, yachts, tax remissions, remissions of sin, hot lines to the almighty. And whole countries. Take 'em, they're yours.

David, we are told, followed the pattern. He learned the handbook, by heart, maybe under the bedclothes as a boy.

And yet, somewhere along the line, something went wrong. When he came to rule, it shortly became apparent that his mind was in a double bind, a situation practically unique among the single minded great. There was a kind of mystical strain in him, a warm steady current in a cold stream of violence, rapacity, kingupmanship. So, he ruled with a divided mind, not entirely macho, not entirely bloody, capable of repentance. This was hell, to have the handbook by heart—but to have a heart divided. David is interesting, even his sins are interesting; a schizoid king, in a job which demands, above all, lock and stock, fidelity to the handbook.

Let us say, to be precise, his sins will be of interest on two accounts. In the first place, he will never sin with the bold-ness required, the set chin, the rectitudinal mouth that knows the shape of its face (kingly), the eyes set on the world like jewels (conscious of their asking price), the brow that wears a crown, and knows it. (Therefore, steady on, we're in the right.)

Not so easy. Uneasy lies this head. David veers. He sins, but he repents. And this is of interest (about which more later). Of interest, one thinks, in proportion as it evades the stereotype.

Then too, David is capable of an intrinsically interesting sin. Beyond rape, so to speak. Beyond his son Solomon, surely one of the most crashing bores of recorded history. Beyond Farouk. Beyond the generals, who replace the kings, clean up the palaces' beds, get rid of the concubines and the hardcore porno, rev up the secret police, put mur-der on a legitimate basis.

Beyond all that, at least now and then, David comes up with something new, something that shows us, if only for a moment, that a finer mind is at work in the world, a mind that sees the world as something more than a pie to be cooked, poisoned, and then hacked up.

David is godly, more than he is kingly. At least now and then. But he is king. And he sees God as a king. And is uneasy.

Competition? He's promethean. He wants the whole pie. Move over God. You've a competitor. I try harder.

So we have a contest worth talking about, worth ponder-ing. Who gives a fig for the kings—Farouk, Solomon, Nich-olas, the Hapsburgs—or the generals who wash away the stains of blood and semen from the palace beds, the palace walls; who conceive murder, with the help of technology, deception, surveillance, and torture—immaculately?

David probes God. He takes no claims for granted. Even God's claims.

And all this is done with the sweetest air imaginable. There is something of the innocent about this king, a child on a throne, a wise child, a cruel child, a passionate youngster; something unspoiled in the midst of the world's stench; something in his gaze is uncorrupted, even while criminal, cunning, rapacious (like all the others). And yet —unlike them, too.

Some center, something upright in the flaccid world of power, whose structure is based on cruelty and force, whose eyes are all seeing, adamant, with no depths. No power of looking inward. Because there is nothing to see, no soul.

David has soul. He's part poet, a harpist, a composer. His songs are his best works, better than his kingship, his battles, his contrivings and diplomacy. Heartrending, tender, fanciful, surreal on occasion, pastoral, worldly, out of the depths, out of a soul with dimension—height, depth. The poet is also a king, the songs imply. The "also" says much.

His sin reaches us across eyes that are attentive to a harp, to music. And across hands that play on that instrument which in its grace, its stretched fibers, is an image of the soul itself. A harpist. He could calm with a song, the murderous moods of Saul, and take the risk (and now and again the event) of a spear throw at his own body. Quite a man.

David's soul aspires to God; to the beauty of the world, to a shepherd's boyhood, to an uncomplicated human ethic, to native goodness and instinctive agape. But he is king. And this is the rub, which rubs his soul raw. And in this, he stands apart finally from others, the crashing bloody boring stereotypes of power. David is himself, interesting —lyrical, torn, skeptical of his own power, capable of conversion to the living.

Then one day he sins, in a way that touches On High.

51

Touches Him where it hurts. For God also is king. And he recoils, troubled, outraged even. Whence comes this sin, a sin which is of interest—to history, to ourselves?

David is an imperialist, for all that he is a mystic. You can't miss the gleam in his eye, of possessions and power; and out of the corner of his eye, the lust for more; for the main chance, the next expedient move, lose one, win two. And like every imperialist, he has to keep an accurate score sheet, if he is to win his next move. How many hoplites, how many sacks of corn, how many palace women, how many men under arms, how many taxpayers, how much cold cash. He decides on a census, in order to get at the most important statistic of all—how large a military levee is possible, and how quickly.

". . . and Joab gave the sum of the number of the people to the king, and there were found of Israel 800,000 valiant men that drew the sword; and of Juda 500,000 fighting men."

Now the Lord was outraged. An earthly king is edging into the tent of the almighty. Into Providence, strictly God's business. Win or lose, it's up to him. Hadn't he given the breath of life to all, isn't their beginning and end in his hands? And what difference between king or chattel slave to him? Except that the king is to be a more visible sign of His kingdom and glory . . .

David had overstepped, he was playing god. And shortly the word came down, he must pay for it.

The punishment is a curious one, involving in fact a choice of punishments; some years of lesser trouble, widespread over the land; some months of danger personal to the king; some terrible days of mass death. "Thus says the Lord; choose which you will; either three years famine, or three months to flee from your enemies, and not to be able to escape their sword; or three days to have the sword of the Lord, and pestilence in the land, and the angel of the

52

Lord destroying in all the coasts of Israel."

An astonishing proposal, indeed. A punishment meted out carefully as to time and victims, finely and cleverly drawn, a kind of three horned dilemma, so to speak. David must choose, a veritable Solomon; choose the least of three evils (which in any case, will still be evil). And the evils come from the hand of the all good, and are, therefore, presumably good for him. Moreover the afflictions are aimed not only at his own sweet skin, but at the people.

A near extermination is proposed. And how many will die in three years of famine? Or in that more intensely stoked furnace of pestilence, how many will die within three short days? And how is David to measure his own life against the lives of thousands of his people?

Now we have suggested that David's imperial itch is the clue to his disease. To have, to hold, to increase his holdings and havings. And more especially, and when the chips are down, the imperialist saves his own skin, the ultimate good of life.

So David falls from the most spectacular sin of all, the sin that makes him interesting and complicated, the sin of an imperial poet—he falls from that, to the stereotyped sin of the imperialist. He gives up his people, to save his own life from his enemies.

His ruminations on the occasion are sublime in their directness, their naive selfishness. " 'I am on every side in a great strait; but it is better for me to fall into the hands of the Lord—for his mercies are many—than into the hands of men.' So the Lord sent a pestilence upon Israel. And there fell of Israel seventy thousand men."

Someone else is doing the body count now, a dolorous business.

But that choice of David! Faith, selfishness, power—what a lethal mix (lethal for those not gifted with the magical triad). For men and women may be faithful, but are mostly powerless; or they may be powerful, but are generally faithless. But David is king, and the king can choose his fate.

Moreover, his choice (to live, to let others die) has the sanction of the almighty, and is, therefore, an act of greater moment, more mysterious, than a merely typical imperial choice. Even if David's choice implies that others are expendable and the king is not, his choice remains in some sense a religious one, a kind of obedience. So we are told.

In any case, David repents, and obeys. And now God will obey him. He will become the king's hangman.

But what of this God? For if we find the king's conduct objectionable, while it flows from a divine proposal, are we not required also to question the conduct of the almighty? Demanding as we must, a morality of our God which is superior to that commonly encountered among earthly rulers?

Was God staking out so difficult a test, hoping against hope (the virtue of the godly) that the king would come through in a personally responsible and unselfish way?

And supposing the king chose to put his own life in danger, to undergo the test of the sword's edge, would he not thereby vindicate the goodness and unselfishness of God, and in its earthly orbit, the goodness of the king?

But beyond these moral whirlwinds, this calculated chaos, a troublesome question arises, what of the people? When do they get to choose? Why was not the proposal made to them instead of David—since presumably they had not sinned, but were being placed by the terms of the proposal, in mortal danger of death, as adjuncts, chattel, possessions. Was not God treating them as mere pawns, their lives a ransom?

Now, undoubtedly, we are showing nothing so clearly as our historical ignorance and psychological naiveté in placing such questions in the way of God and his servant David. Experts will point out the quasi-divine aura that surrounded the king, the advantage of his easy access to the almighty, as well as his necessary mediating office. Though, perhaps, these excusing factors suffer somewhat as to underpinnings when we think of the prophets who hung around on the margin of favor and disgrace, willy nilly shoving the unpalatable truth at the imperialists.

Or again we will be reminded that the "people" until very recently were a voiceless mass, that to die by pestilence was no unusual thing in torrid climates, that the idea of "choosing one's fate" is a very recent one, that we are attempting to democratize a different age, etc.

To which one responds; if it would seem a good idea to be able to choose for oneself, one's family, one's town, survival or death—if this is a good and human thing—then it would seem fitting that God conceive the idea a little ahead of ourselves.

Indeed, has any choice been made, until I have chosen for myself, and the people for themselves? And presupposing grace, love, energies available—is it not required that all these be available to us, as well as to a king? And most of all, that in matters closely touching life and death and the common welfare, the people be heard from? And is it not true that, short of such a hearing, there can be no talk of serious social change, or of a revolution—or, indeed more modestly, of a religion worthy of human beings?

Our moral; we are not meant to be permanently in tutelage.

A sign of the moral violation both of nature and divine love, is that others choose for us. For their own good, as is said. In such a way, we petrify the adolescent in childishness, and ourselves in the cycle of David's sin; which is, we lord it over others, first by a body count, and then by a bloody forfeit. That is to say, the overlord first reduces humans to possessions. And then, since possessions are weighed against other possessions, he gives up the people to death, whenever the supreme good is at stake, viz, that skin which is rarer and dearer than all the world (his own skin).

Perhaps, in this welter of blood, ego, and contrary claims, God too can be forgiven. Perhaps, his activity is subtler, more human so to speak, than a first reading of the story allows. Perhaps, he acts somewhat like the producer of a drama, entitled "The Body Count of King David," staging the text, enabling its appearance. Insisting in fact that murder go public. Dramatizing this fact; that people, ordinary people, poor people, are always and everywhere expendable, a crude constant of history. Indeed, but for a few examples offered by the saints, people are the first expendable objects of this world. They exist for no other reason than to be bought, sold, exploited, degraded; they die and kill for others, they are employed or unemployed as integers in service to the dollar; they steal what joy they know, as an extracurricular, a benefit for having their most precious parts, their freedom, their tongues, their dignity, their cheerfulness and even temper—all of these amputated at birth. Little indeed is left to them of the promise, the patrimony. Neither birth right, nor life right, nor happiness right, nor freedom right. Only a death right.

Now this wiping out of humans by kings has by no means ended with the death of kings. Which goes without saying. Human expendability has only been transformed, simplified, technologized, has learned a new jargon, is now, so to speak, a spiritualized savagery. Our scene is the modern world. Give up your mind, give up your soul, give up your conscience. We are generous; we will spare you what is left.

Now most of us would prefer, could we call the shots, to have all this proceed in private, or under cover; the latest diplomacy, the latest duplicity. And this is where God insists on being useful; quite out of character. He wants to unmask the heart of the king. He is uneasy that the king can be now a poet, now a killer; and make the former the mask, the excuse, the vindication of the latter. Multiple roles displease him, when life and death are at stake, and when the roles tend, not to cancel one another out, but to blur the true and main intent of rampageous ego. So he says, choose. Famine, personal death, public extermination. What he is truly saying is, choose publicly, since your heart has already chosen in private. You have chosen violence over compassion, hatred over community, possessions over persons, war over peace, yourself over me. Now I will show you what you are and, in the showing, many will die. For this is what it is to be king, this is the true meaning of that power you lust after, and accrue. Let the curtain go up. The play's the thing wherein I'll catch the conscience of the king.

Now I would not have us let off easily, as though to say these are hard words, thank God they are about David, or thank God they are about powers and principalities. Thank God they are at distance from me.

They are not at distance from me. The claim is premature, self-blinded. The words are true of the powerful, they are also true of the powerless—at least of those powerless who aspire in their misery, to the same power as their oppressor. And, therefore, inevitably, aspire to the method of the oppressor. A like murder, a like ego, a like duplicity, a like malice, a like pride, a like covetousness. A like world, in spite of the rhetoric about a new world. The same bloody world, botched by the same bloody sword. So what is new, so what is ever new?

I take hope because the words are at distance at least from a few. The words about David are true, invariably, depressingly, predictably, of those in power. They count us, they give us up, they save themselves. And the words about David are true, invariably, depressingly, predictably, of the

57

envious who are without power. They would like to count us, they would like to give us up, they would like to save themselves.

But not true of all. Not of one, not of a few. This is my body which is given for you. This is the cup of my blood, which is shed for you and for all, that murder may be turned around. This is a sign of a new and everlasting friendship. Every time you eat this body and drink this blood, turn power around, turn envy around, turn powerlessness around. Turn murder around, turn history around. Toward me.

The Whale's Tale

I have a man inside me
like the universe.

It all seemed like the most natural thing in the world. To begin with, a day of utmost beauty. I was steaming along on my own, a cloudless blue sky, the sea trackless and shimmering; an impressive argument for, so to speak, the providence of God.

Then, with shocking suddenness and no prior consultation, a storm overhead. Well, I reflected swallowing hard, what, after all, is a storm to me. It merely heightens the joy and variety of the course—like running through a great forest instead of a mowed field. Blowing and spinning, sending up clouds of steam, I plow along, in wonderment at the harsh grandeur of the primary weather. Waves that break and form again, momentary cliffs; I leap off one, carried along on the tip of another, the waters in perpetual ecstasy, forming, dissolving, taking shape, breaking up. So caught up in life, the waters like ecstatic dancers, moment by moment tossing aside, assuming their guises.

Then, like a thunderclap, ahead of me, trouble.

A ship wallowing and limping along, half its yards sheared away.

What a scupperful of fools, I snorted, out on such a day.

59

They have all the earth for their own, what more do they want?

But for all my annoyance, cursed with my great heart I kept drawing near, alongside or in her wake; though it was hard work, indeed, keeping that tortured mote in view through so monstrous a vortex.

In regard to them, I know only one law; when things are bad, there's worse to come. As though a ship in distress weren't enough to contend with, there's the sailors. With them, you never know what's going to happen, once folly takes over. I've seen them scuttle a perfectly sound ship and leap into the void in sieves one tenth the size of the decks they jump from. They pray to their gods, you see them shivering and yelling on deck, on their knees no less—and you know it; anything can happen. I've seen them dance around in a frenzy, then break off, break away, leap overboard, deck, then air, sea, never loosening their grip on one another.

Now I was closer. They were praying all right. The marathon was on. I pulled nearer.

Kneeling in a circle on a deck, a poor water-soaked bundle in their midst; they were attending to it with the ominous devotion that always precedes some horrible move, something religious. Three of them picked him up, unresisting (he was probably religious, too). The others stood there in the fury of wind, the storm coming at them horizontal, demons tossing brimstone in their faces. Arms raised, faces a concentrated horror, they stumbled toward the railing of that foundering scow, imprecating, the unresisting bundle dragged along. A burial at sea, they were burying him alive!

Oh I know their ilk, they and their gods. Why should they give a sou about one another? Their religion forbids it.

They threw him over, to hell and gone.

60

And I caught the bundle of misery neatly on a fluke, tossed it forward to a flipper.

Held him up there, like a newborn babe, eye to eye. Who was this castaway? A prophet?

When that suspicion dawned, I almost pulled in my life-saving equipment and let him go down. Trod water there only half believing my eyes.

How'd I know who he was? I didn't for certain. But in our line of work, and given our age on earth, the chances were overwhelming. We're always being called on to save their chestnuts. The bestiary of providence—whales, porpoises, ravens, lions, jackasses even. Prophets loud as thunder on the saving word, short as sticks on consequences. No, they rush forward, despise the anger, danger, bad-mouthing, death even. Onward Christian soldiers! That's their disease, it's called glory.

Well, there I was, this morsel of misery on the end of my flipper, blinking back at me like the day of his birth. Storm blowing doomsday, rising and falling in unison, a mad madrigal. A prophet, I knew it. It could only be.

They all look—how to put it?—like the half-drowned cat that just swallowed the half-dead canary. Not exactly living, better off than dead. He sat there hanging on, a steady look, a mouse in a cat's cradle. He knew all along I'd be hanging about, just waiting for the sublime privilege of plucking him from the sea; that salvation look, unmelting, unto himself, beyond circumstance.

I saw it in his eyes. When they tossed him into the drenched air like a corpse in its canvas—he didn't care a whit! That's what his look said, louder than words. He didn't care; there might be nothing between him and salty oblivion, or there might be a whale's right arm to pluck him out of the sea.

Why should he care? There was always an option. Savior

whale, killer sea, that wasn't all there was. I shouldn't get
overbearing. What greater privilege for a mere whale anyway, than to save the Lord's anointed?

Of course, we're supposed to be at their beck, snatching
them from ruin. By such a neat arrangement they wipe out
at a stroke the heroism, the coolheadedness, the near miraculous benignity, of our vocation. And in the process, cano-
nize their own vagaries. Behold, the Lord's handpicked can
do no wrong!

This one wasn't exactly jaunty, though. After all, he'd
had a shakeup, his future was uncertain. But he was confi-
dent! Neck deep in innocence. He hadn't lived long
enough to realize what a triphammer life is, beating you out
of one shape, into another.

His first adventure; he was like an infant tossed between
playful adults. Younger than I, by a century or so, no beard,
eyes too big to qualify for the world. He looked more like
the captain's boy than the captain; all the harder to reason
with.

Well, this was the conversation that followed, I swear it.

By no means repenting his situation, he began: "Good
day, sir." Oh he was cool. Here we were only half in this
world, a small chip on the back of a large one, both caught
in a tidal wave, and he wished me a good day, sir!

——I thank you for your service this day. You have
saved me from a watery end. (Which minus the cliche was
the naked truth.)

——Blameless as I am, I was tossed overboard by hea-
then sailors. They know no better, as you are aware, being
worshippers of false gods. (Couldn't resist rolling out his
big guns on me, perched a half-inch from the abyss as he
was, totally dependant on me for the salvation of his limbs.
Improve me he would!)

——You may be sure you have won a great blessing by
your saving action, he blared.

——You have preserved a servant of the true God, who rewards and punishes according to our service and his good pleasure. Blah blah. A fundamentalist to the end. Drowned he might be, or near it, from his chattering teeth to his blue toe nails. But his tongue? Limber to the end.

Did I call it a conversation? People like him don't hold conversations, they rent auditoriums, even the open sea and its tempests are not safe from their great lungs. What could I do, but blink in disbelief and take my medicine like the good beast I am?

A pause in his confabulations, while he gathered breath from the winds. I interjected, the first sensible remark of the exchange.

——And what would you suggest we do now? The question was not for him at all; it was addressed to the only sensible being in sight—myself.

What was I to do? Land him safe on some distant shore, a polyp on a platter? But we were nowhere near a shore; in the full rage of the sea, God had let go of him, midway, so to speak, between unwelcome sky and bottomless wave. Jonah could point his prophetic finger where his fancy pleased: north, east, south, west, go here, run there, it was all equidistant; he was nowhere. We wouldn't make it; or more properly, he wouldn't. Not soaked and frozen in the extremities and half gone with hunger as he was.

Now with such serious issues at hand, I didn't like his preaching, finding it among other deficiencies redundant, badly composed and untimely. But that doesn't mean let me add, that I'm theologically hostile. How could I be, plunged as I am in a watery world that even a blind shark could see is more laden with design than chance?

We whales have been around a long time. We may not have leather lunged prophets to tell us the cosmic score. Maybe we don't need them. Nor, might I add, do we on

63

occasion, carve them into sections, cast them overboard in storms, or crucify them to trees.

Anyway you learn patience. Take life as it comes, step by step. Granted for a moment God signaled to me that morning; follow such and such a ship, they're making gull fodder out of my chosen, and I want it stopped. Granted he set the compass and synchronized the clocks. (Granted on the other hand, he also set the barometer plunging.) I'm willing to waive the argument because the moment is a pressing one; viz, I've got the *Vox Dei* hanging on to me as though I'm the everlasting arms. Now what do I do?

Obviously, he's in no state to make a suggestion worth listening to; and hearken as I may, I hear no divine voice twitching at my ear lobe, telling me the next move.

So what *is* to be done?

There's not a moment to be lost. He's got a look in his eye like a poster on a picket line; WHALE STEAKS FOR JESUS! (Did you know, by the way, we have bigger brains than they do?) I can all but read his next thought; no great feat, he gives it away, sitting there, counting off on his fingers the proofs for the existence of God most apt to win a waterlogged pachyderm to the one true way.

I had enough. Pursed my lips a bit, leaning in his direction, as though rendered thoughtful by his wisdom, about to share a confidence out of earshot of the almighty.

And took him in like a smelt. Swallowed. He went down easy . . .

JONAH, ARE YOU DOWN THERE?

He heard me all right. We're among the few mammals who can reverse their voice box. This unique gift of inward rumination is granted for just such occasions, when we've suddenly had to swallow a prophet for his own good.

JONAH—ARE YOU . . . ?

O I knew he was there. You see, we can also reverse our

eyesight, in order to check on inward operations, so to speak.

Oh, he wasn't fooling me with his silence. I could see him crouching in a corner of my guest suite, in a low mood I judged. I couldn't see his face too well, he being too miffed even to light the candle I had thoughtfully provided on a shelf. (Along I might add, with basic survival foods, central heating, soft wall to wall membrane; even, if he required sleep, a folded lap rug. These perquisites snatched from a shipwreck some years before, never ingested or eliminated in view of just such a contingency.)

Ingratitude, in face of all this forethought, these Class A accommodations? You get used to it.

JONAH . . . !

He's humiliated, he's confused. No wonder he's withdrawn. Imagine, a whale for weathervane, world mother, lifeboat—providence! All his choices are gone. The planet's given him up; he's overboard. No one wants him, no one gives a damn.

I'm in charge. That comes down hard on the prophetic spleen.

No idea where he's going, how he's to get there. No sailors, no compass, no captain. No night, no day. No wonder he's unstrung, sleepless, pacing up and down, up and down my guts. Or tossing himself into a corner in a snit. I'm not his proper environment, he's lost all vim, stopped composing sermons. Even given up converting me—the last thing to go, their flagrant apostolic fervor. Well.

Sleep then, Jonah!

Sleep my son, my child.

My whole being, my breast, my womb is for you.

Sleep Jonah in the belly of a paradox. Now you need have no purpose, nothing to prove, nowhere to go.

You may, as of now, stop talking, stop planning, stop

thinking. The God who thinks of you has no need of your thought. The God who loves you has no need of your love. The God who upholds the universe has no need of your strength.

Why should he? Are you then to hold him up?

Sleep Jonah, in a motion that is no motion, in a direction that is no direction. Does the unborn child order its mother about, when to sit, when to eat, when to go forth, what words to speak? Be still, then, and know that I am God.

There will be a time perhaps (perhaps!) when these things will be proper, in accord with right reason. But only when you have been born again; if, indeed, you are to be born, which event is not in your devising either.

Be still, Jonah, sleep at last. (He sleeps at last.) In the belly of your savior, in the perilous, fathomless sea, where salvation is a miracle and death is most likely—sleep.

Let me whisper to you, prophet, maker, doer, voyager, weaver of words, serious browed one, rambunctious, moody one. There is one greater than you, and he is silent. There is one who encompasses you, and he lets you go. There is one named Hope, and he casts you overboard. There is one named God and his servant is—a whale.

Embryo, sleeper, mote, pin prick, blind eye, pretender, blusterer. Sleep awhile, awaken and rub your eyes; then perhaps he will summon you.

Until then, I bear you through the pathless sea. Another than you plans for you, another than you breathes for you, another than you loves you, another than you sees before and after, yesterday and tomorrow. While you lie there, ignorant of where you come from, where you might be going, indeed, of who you are.

Who am I, you will ask on awakening, as your eyes open, as the light floods in, as you walk the earth once more. As over you floats, and then entwines, over shoulders and arms and legs and close about your head, the cloak of import, the cloak of office, the cloak so ample you must stand upright in order to wear it properly, and walk about to show it to best advantage, and speak sonorously to draw attention to its splendor. Why, this is my cloak, I am Jonah the prophet, man of the truth, man burdened with the world's weight, the world's sin, the world's error. And you will twitch your mantle, impatient for time lost, you world-encompassing man, and make a noise in public once more, and breathe deep while the people cry; Jonah, the prophet of the most high is in our midst; hearken to him, repent!

And you will forget the days and nights you passed in the belly of a whale, in the belly of absurdity, in the belly of birth.

You great man! Only remember; once for a space you shuddered on the tip of a mortal dilemma out of which you were drawn by no power of your own, by no word of yours, by the unlikely flipper of a whale.

Sent to save you.

No archangel.

Not Providence.

Not a prophet.

Not God.

Behold! A wallowing insensate ugly fog-hued oversized paradigm of the inscrutable ways.

He wakens

in me

my son, Jonah.

The Curse

The curse, laid on David, that most blessed among men.

As though he were not in trouble enough! As though the one who leveled the curse had the dignity of a prophet (whereas he was an obscure relative of Saul, a no one set in the king's path, a scandal).

And what was the substance of the curse in any case, compared with the misfortune in which David stood, the crowning shame of betrayal by his own son?

The king has wisdom enough to admit the truth; the curse is nothing more or less than the dark side of his fate, already being enacted. He lies under a curse from birth, from the day of accession to the crown; he is a "man of blood." The unlikely hostile crier of hate is spelling out a truth of the king's existence. To be a king is to be cursed. It is to invite betrayal by those nearest one's love; it is to live by blood-letting, to inherit an account of blood, to walk in blood, and so to increase the account in one's lifetime; it is to pass on the miasma, the curse, the blood accounting, to one's heirs.

David knows the truth. So he neither harms nor hinders the shouter of curses. He goes on his way, laid out for him by his betrayer and son; a way which will only be turned around by the death of Absolom.

As David was reaching Bahurim, out came a man of the
same clan as Saul's family. His name was Shimel son of
Gera, and as he came he uttered curse after curse and
threw stones at David and at all King David's officers,
though the whole army and all the champions flanked the
king right and left. The words of his curse were these, "Be
off, be off, man of blood, scoundrel! Yahweh has brought
on you all the blood of the House of Saul whose
sovereignty you have usurped; and Yahweh has transferred
that same sovereignty to Absalom your son. Now your
doom has overtaken you, man of blood that you are."
Abishai son of Zeruiah said to the king, "Is this dead dog
to curse my lord the king? Let me go over and cut his head
off." But the king replied, "What business is it of mine and
yours, sons of Zeruiah? Let him curse. If Yahweh said to
him 'Curse David,' what right has anyone to say, 'Why
have you done this?' " David said to Abishai and all his
officers, "Why, my own son, sprung from my body, is now
seeking my life; so now how much the more this
Benjaminite? Let him curse on if Yahweh has told him to.
Perhaps Yahweh will look on my misery and repay me with
good for his curse today." (2 Samuel, 16:5–12)

The quality of David! He turns his head meekly to one side,
and takes the brunt of a mean spirit, vengefulness, hatred,
fractiousness, malice, evil joy in the fall of the great—a
hundred base motives, mixed motives. The man has a truth
to tell, in spite of all. And he is heard.

Pure are the ears, indeed, and attuned to reality, that can
discern the truth under all this debris, falsehood, fear.

The king must have known in the depths of his soul, that
he, his line, his "system," had set the stage for tragedy. The
stage was set on a cart, a moveable show; and the cart was
on a slope. The way, from every moral and human point of
view, was down hill.

The curse is the other side of the blessing. One who has
never been cursed has quite probably never been blessed.

That is what saves. From pride, from self love, from

becoming God's bully boy. Such a person, blessed in a most ambiguous way, knowing nothing of the other side of life, the side of the dispossessed, the victims, the losers—he goes about, a stalking curse. His existence turns into a curse. And it is laid on others, more often than not.

The likely truth in unlikely places, coming from unsuspected lips.

It widens into a historical method that seems to make sense of things. You get one side of things, then you get the other side. In consequence, you step up, or away, or down; but into a different stance. Then you get—not a third side, but a kind of whole picture, as though finally two sides of a coin came together or the convex and concave of a single mirror. It takes time, and patience.

The king is a dog. If you meet the Buddha, kill him. Cut off the finger of the one who points to the truth. Everything "religious" has about it a sense of the iconoclastic, as the Zen Buddhists know. Break the false images. Especially, break those which come at you with 14-karat credentials.

Whose life today has about it the aura of a curse? Whose of a blessing? The question is a fiercely contended one, the contrary claimants to God's favor are legion. But very few submit to the curse, in the manner of David, very few could bear hearing it uttered. Fewer still who would not urge condign punishment on the one who uttered it.

Meantime, churches rush to bless the state, in the full and bloody exercise of death.

And the state, a quasi-church in its own right, endowed with pomp, liturgies, incantations, persuasive language, hypocrisy, ties in knots and double knots the consciences of citizens. The state also has its blessing, and confers it with rigor and austere care. The state has been known even to bless the church.

71

What form though, might the blessing of God take, when genuinely conferred? We are speaking, of course, of a symbolic order of things, a right karma. An at-one-ment with the universe of matter and spirit. Creatureliness. Certain classical attitudes which crop up blessedly so to speak, in all times and cultures, breaking through the underbrush of lust after possessions, cruelty, blindness, the generational diseases of the human lot.

We are speaking of nothing magical. Though just as certainly we are speaking of something mystical. I want with all my heart, to taste God in a sense that evades all words, to "live to tell of it." Forever.

At the same time, I want to live among people and things. Not in a crazy grasping consuming way certainly. (But describe the right way!)

One whose life as blessed confers a blessing on others. On the other hand, there is the permeating sadness of David, turning away from the one who cursed him. The best the king can do, in the presence of—what? The transcendent, the inapprehensible, the divine bearing down on him, is, if he is wise and temperate (rarely) and even lucky, is— to turn away. Not, at least, to answer in kind. David recoils, he is struck to the heart. It can be said of him (no mean praise, applied to the powerful) he knows a curse when he hears one.

But what is to be done then? Flee the scene, fast, in silence. David, who fled the curse as though it were a malign magnetic field, still could not confer a blessing. He was a man of power, of blood, of this world. His grace (which in the powerful is bound to be minimal) was, at least, to know this, to know his karma.

The Curse

There is the curse of God, and there is the curse of the state. The strategy of the latter is to announce itself as the oracle of the former. By such an inspired tactic, the morally illiterate and fear ridden are reduced to ashes, quickly. Their inability to separate out the word of God from the word of Caesar, comes down on them like a universal solvent, lye, acid, dissolution. Dry bones.

The curse of the state is the proclamation that the citizen (delinquent or deviant) is in a wrong karmic stance, "out of it." What "it" is, is, of course, constant, well defined, well testified to, greatly audible throughout national history; the thunder of goose stepping cits. The curse declares that one is out of step. Watch it!

Out of step with reality. This is the tremendous, straight-faced, emboldened, constant indictment. It is brought down year after year, century after century, by the impassive, utterly self-confident phalanx of alterns, subalterns, battle ribbons, bifocals, boots, saddles, masks, helmets, advisors, visors, coveralls, barks, commands, clarifications, stumblings and bumblings, threats, hints, outright lies, downright half truths, speeches, banquets, reprisals, tapes, documents, top secrets—in fact (and the telling leaves one limp with the irony) by the same "authority" today as always. Stale bread, cruel circuses.

Well. Out of step. Cursed also by God, as his high priests testify (at least by their prudent boot licking silence). They know well how to come down hard, those twin myrmidons. Beware, faint of heart. Get out fast.

Any principality of this world had, in degree, the power to curse. That is, it can place under the decree of exclusion or condemnation, anyone who defies its "values," proposes to live by contrary values; or who, simply for one arbitrary reason or another, can't quite make it. Or doesn't want to.

But the biggest Brother of them all is beyond doubt that behemoth, clawed and armor plated, known in children's bedtime stories as the imperial nation state. This is the proper ape of God, miming his governance of the world. How? It creates, annexes, concocts, technologizes, a kingdom on which mortal sun never sets, a tin can paradise, a nest of unassuageable appetites. Then it proceeds to announce that citizenship in its precincts is the highest human good, the most fertile field of growth, privilege, honor, of human and civil rights. And finally, this secular inflation receives, on the part of most, the response for which it hankered all the while; a properly religious awe. "They cried out, who is like to the beast? . . . and the whole world followed after the beast. . . ."

The occasion is probably near, if it has not already arrived, when one will be required to endure the curse of both church and state—as the price of God's blessing.

Such a statement should not be made idly, lightly. Nor is it so made here.

One sign that the times are ripening toward such an occasion; blessings are conferred cheaply, large handedly, by both church and state, on the pusillanimous self-multiplying undifferentiated soldier-citizen-believers who frequent in turn, the sanctuary of each power: battlefield, temple, polling place.

But, it might reasonably be asked, what do such blessings mean? The people have followed the piper into the side of the mountain. Then it closes. The children have vanished forever.

The blessing of God, rightly understood, often arrives in the form of a curse. In some such way, Jesus we are told, was declared "anathema" by God. Abandoned. He was

74

denied all appeal; the decree of the state stood firm, and was executed.

He was abandoned also in the sense of mystical support, of strength in dark hours; that mouth-to-mouth respiration which the Spirit grants to lovers and friends.

No understanding without irony. Deep, deep under, Job curses his life, his birth, the moment of his conception. Nausea with existence. Then he surfaces from his deep filthy mine, blear-eyed, black with the core sediment of the earth; something mysterious clutched in his palm. And a smile, a smile to stop the stars in their courses. A lowly miner of coal, he has come on—diamonds.

The one who curses another is hobnobbing with death.

In several senses. First because cursing is a kind of incantation of (and in that sense, a tribute to) the realm of death. In summoning the power of death, in so "fingering" the guilty, one is, in a true sense, asking for it himself. Death bows to no master save God; short of Him, its malice is without limit.

Then too, the curse belongs only to the realm of faith. It makes no sense to curse the world, which already, according to Paul, lies under the curse. So Jesus reserves his anathemas for false religious leaders; he has no such language for Pilate.

The curse is a last ditch measure; it presupposes the exhaustion of all other remedies. This is what makes it so terrifying; it belongs only to the "last days." Then the works of God, his words, will have beaten in vain against portals that are blind, locked, sunken in vanity. Miracles as well; unavailing. A situation barely imaginable; a blindness beyond anything one could attribute to "normal" folly. Then, this thundrous cry from the mouth of God.

Certain artifacts can be understood only as evidence of the curse of God. Instruments of modern war, methods of torture, psychological invasion and tinkering, slum properties, crematoria for the living; today one should add prisons, mental hospitals, stockpiles of nuclear weaponry.

Anything that claims to be God. It was such property and method that some resisters castigated in the sixties as "having no right to exist." Experts of all sorts, from U.S. prosecutors to ethical pundits, were equally outraged; the message had gotten through.

The nation that cultivates, builds, maintains, proliferates, experiments in such grotesqueries, is already doomed. There is no special need of a voice from Sinai to say so. As for those who consider themselves non-consumers of fallout, they had best "flee to the hills."

One of the loveliest blessings of all time is chanted by three youths, condemned to death, in the very act of execution. "Sirach, Misach and Abdenago . . . walked about in the flames, singing to God and blessing the Lord. These three in the furnace with one voice singing, glorifying and blessing God."

State curse, divine blessing. Together, fused in conflict, stoked, set afire. How unlikely it is on the face of it, that the condemned, wiped out by decree of the state, should still summon this superfluity, this sublime overflow of life, this poetry of existence endangered!

A curse is a kind of proclamation of a reality; today's announcement of yesterday's bad news. News which up to today, so to speak, has not been known. More, has been willfully concealed, by all kind of staged, duplicitous, formal, stiffnecked, debased, rote, conduct. Prior to the curse, or apart from it, secular life (or church life) proceeds with an appalling normality. "In the days of Noah, they ate and drank, married and gave in marriage." And for all its trouble, Chicken Little had its neck wrung.

The priest is one who blesses; he is reminded of it on the day of ordination. And yet, one cannot help reflect with a twinge of sadness, how many of these pages have been given over to equivalent curses! As though, indeed, the universe were a badly concocted, twin-yolked egg; one part polluted, one part fertile. No such gnostic nightmare! The blessing is for *all* of life, all of it; the blessing is already there, like a waterspout twisting between heaven and earth, like a fiery umbilical between the sun and ourselves, like the other side of the Other Side. Like bread and wine.

On the day men and women accept themselves as accursed, in a great twist of revulsion, the earth will go up in flames. That day, the curse will be, as they say, "internalized."

What a contrast with the Day announced by God's gentle and majestic Son. On that day, the blessing of creation, the hymn of existence, the lives and deaths of his faithful ones, and how much more—all this will be "internalized." Maranatha; come, Lord Jesus.

The Patience of Job
in Detroit, Michigan

He was a slight inauspicious man, chain smoking deep into his cancerous guts. His misfortunes were notable, even for our world.

Alone, unmarried, he adopted two black children; twenty years after one was a mental patient, the other a heroin addict.

Of late, Demos passed almost a year in a hospital; half his insides are now outside. He returned to Stoepel, a street of small brick houses of the type Detroit xeroxes to the horizon. And found he had been the object of a sublime, consummated ripoff. The second story flat, rented to a young couple, was a shambles; everything that would fetch a buck was torn loose, transported, sold, fenced. Four walls, not very clean, greeted his eyeballs. The tenants had vanished.

Start over. He started over. When I arrived on the scene, seeking shelter in Detroit midwinter, he received me without enthusiasm. You'll stay only three months? After that, I go looking for another tenant? No thank you.

Later that day he phoned. I could come.

Perhaps it was only that losers flock together. Or perhaps losers clone themselves into more losers. In any case, I was shortly inducted as a member of the home team that has not won a round, let alone a game, in anyone's memory.

The instance is nothing new. I was now a Detroit loser, from being a New York loser, a Winnipeg loser, a Danbury loser, a Paris loser, a Tel Aviv . . . enough.

He had that look of the aging cat that can still swallow birds; a bad diet for cancer, feathers and all. But in consequence, could he sing, could he talk, could he philosophize and meander and ruminate and expostulate and . . .

He used to wait for me as I came in at the front door; from there, it was strictly run for the stairs! But that was an empty gesture if he wanted me, he had me, bird in the snare, for hours.

A talker! No wonder the book of Job goes on and on; these types make talk a substitute for lost life; that way, one lives practically forever.

Mostly about his misfortunes, of course. What else was there?

In the hospital he'd had a dream, Greek Catholic. Saints Cosmas and Damian, whose silver framed ikon was on the mantel, appeared to him in sleep one night; his house was full of blood, but they announced a clean up. And by dawn, the house was clean. And he did recover.

There was nothing to do but take the dream symbolically; that way he could avoid the brute fact; his house, first floor, was a shambles.

The recovery didn't work either. Troubles multiplied like Job's boils. One day he had all but four or five of his pestiferous teeth yanked. Thereafter, for almost a week, the poor scare crow was alight with fever, a sign to the nations. His doctor, some miles distant at Ann Arbor, wanted him back for retooling; not knowing whether our friend was harboring another cancerous flare, or whether his sore gums were inflamed. Antibiotics, in any case, restored him; not to health (that was out of the question) to less immanent death.

Two mongrel pups had the run of the back yard; they reduced the outdoor space to roughly the same chaos as the inside. You had to give it to him, a morbid consistency around and within.

The dogs also yapped all night, for no given reason. And we, in the classic standoff of landlord and serf, had words.

Then there was a question of the heat, which he controlled, part of the rent package, a mild ripoff. He rationed me, one coal at a time, so to speak, a poorhouse beadle. More words.

There was this sublimely irrational thing; Job was downstairs, so to speak, inhabiting his dung heap, and by hook, crook, dog, and thermostat, creating another misery, in his own image, upstairs.

A two-tiered universe, the Greek church fathers' doctrine of "eikons," the platonic supersensible forms. I used to draw for (cold) comfort, on this or that half-buried half-forgotten symbol. Was I his ideal supernal transcendental Loser, under wraps, like Lazarus? Lord let me out!

I came to see, our upper and lower berths were an image of the universe. To wit, it was metaphysically impossible for me to do the simplest thing well or rightly. If he came up the stairs and I let him in, willy nilly he had nothing on his mind but words, a velleity, a spate of waste. I was an ear, to be rinsed by the hour. And if I crouched there at the books and held my peace when he knocked at the door, ignoring him, disaster was sure to follow.

One day, sick and weak as water, (as I learned later to my utmost chagrin) he scarcely made the stairs, knocked, heard only silence, staggered down again and out of doors for help, fell in the snow, was finally rescued by a neighbor woman.

My state of soul, when I learned this, was roughly that of a whipped cur. I carry those welts to this day.

The world can be awry, and still limp on in its course. There is always a door to be opened, they don't have us quite. In one's dwelling, in one's soul, enough capital good luck dwells that one can dole out a few concessions, can bear with God, can find in solitude and meditation and sleep and books, a healing the world neither creates nor dispenses.

Another way of saying, of course, that we are still on page one and a half of our reading of the book of Job. Satan, that stalking adversary, has yet another card to play. The card is electronic; pushed in a slot it gives access to the dwelling.

His black pals used to gather in the flat below and play music. Sometimes there were sounds of conflict. But one night the pot boiled over. A mighty fracas struck the walls. I rushed down, to find my diminutive dominie crouching in a corner, over him a great black shadow and its substance, wrestling out of his skinny grasp, the keys of the house.

Demos was screaming like a banshee; the Greek curses are classic, indeed. The black was on a heroin high. It was not a moment to resist. I could only advise, above the tumult, that he hand over the keys, in hopes of preserving his life.

The back door was torn from its bolts. The invader departed, but he now had free access; to us, to our possessions. Satan, though numbered among the sons of God, is still adversary, the tester, the withholder, the ripoff artist of the cosmos, footpad, cat thief.

Addict?

He came back, and back. With a woman, also addicted, two bewildered hangdog children (imagine their fate). All in a battered tin monster that should have been lettered, as they were christened, *Spirit of Detroit.*

When Demos was out, they'd batter at the front door, spitefully, I thought; honkey come on down, let us in. Though they had keys to the back door. Where's mah fathah?

The Patience of Job in Detroit, Michigan

I didn't know, I never knew anything, not wheah's mah welfah check? Wheah's mah mail? Wheah's them dawgs? I knew nothing, the ironically correct answer for a skull like me, I don't know, anything, I work at the university. They'd go snapping and shuffling through the house, the children hanging listless as ragdolls from the burnt out chariot. Upstairs I'd wait their next move. With dread; sometimes they were high as saturn.

The woman would climb the stairs, too, a tiny simian face, eyes like a monkey's with electrodes in its skull. A carry out coffee in her hand, trembling. Wheah's the ol' man gone to? She asked it, but she didn't know she asked it. I told her, knowing none of it would stick, I don't have the faintest, I'm at school all day. She turned like a stick on its point, like a sleepwalker on a signal, and went down.

There was always time, after such encounters, to sit, weak of knee, and think things out. How did I perform, a question for one's soul, always on tryout, the night before opening night. Panic? Cold sweats? Of course, but then, what are you afraid of losing?

Two things I didn't want: to walk out on the old man, now in hospital indefinitely, and to call the cops. In Detroit, like everywhere, cops add chaos to violence. I'd take my chances.

Alone in the house. They have the keys to the house. I've also promised to protect the old man's social security check. Will do. What I'm in, is a bootcamp in non-violence. In the most violent city in the world. Welcome adversary.

Here comes that old vehicular nightmare chugging into the drive again, like day of judgment. It has a red right fender, like an old warrior's leg painted for battle. The rest is, charitably speaking, baby blue.

Our warrior, young, eases out on the street side. Splay feet, dirty rainbow pants, overweight, a fat truculent face, eyes muddy, far off. He's hot onto that check, but I, in the

83

biblical phrase, have preveniently prevented him, removing said object, a scandal unto his path. What he can't take won't hurt him.

He doesn't know where mah fathah is. In more ways than one. Are you also a hideaway?

I'm not going to push that line, "fathah," no matter how spelled or spelled out. Indeed, isn't the pushing of an image, a line, a superior product, one clue to the barren intransient futility of the Debate Team that gathers around Job? They can't win, they don't have the wit, so they lose, and lose badly, a theological convention in heat.

Meantime, what does God do? He hedges. He plays about. He feints and lunges. He takes chances. He sings songs; he reports up front on the most unlikely and, indeed, outrageous activity of his common life.

He actually *enjoys* his work, and dares say so. It's criminal. He won't be cornered. To answer their bad spirit, to adopt their method, to play their game—it's like four walled handball, an hour or so of diversion. But if you live on the courts, if the ball always mathematically, predictably, returns and arcs out, if its vector and curves are (at least in the abstract) knowable in advance—etc., etc., why then, the world must be put together in the same way. And ourselves. And why not God?

The imagination is the way out of the box. The imagination—the nearest equivalent, in us, to that voice which thunders, sings low, pleads, fulminates, instructs, conveys scorn and affection, fury and serenity.

The unanswerable argument, of course, is to offer no argument. A change of method, a change of pace. He's a butterfly before a bulldozer. No method at all; that madness which is method.

The maker of the universe, the justifier of the universe. Should not the one who got the whole thing in motion, be *responsible*—for its tics and imbalances, its gargantuan irrationality, all of it? Then how about that sovereign side-swipe, the paw that can kill a man? Be silent, and know that I am God.

They don't know how to be silent, the learned argufiers. They don't know that in refusal, that cloud of deliberately induced unknowing, lies wisdom, a road, a fruitful search whose vista is the soul's proper atmosphere: ignorance, the climate of creatureliness.

I heard it now and again, I saw it in the eyes of that dying old guy, who as far as I could judge, had taken swipe after swipe from Leo's wide-ranging right limb—and called it Providence. Imagine. He called the following "Providence": illness unto death, theft of possessions, drug abuse, madness of those he loved, invasion of the house. What was there left to lose? He was a necromancer of the divine. He smiled back at the smile. He beat God at his own game; accepted the errant rules, the unpredictability, the veers and false starts, the game that to all intents went nowhere, could go nowhere, in this world.

The perfect game after all, the game for the sake of the game. In which winning and losing are irrelevant, indeed, corrupting accretions, out of the culture, the cult of "religion."

He cursed the day of his birth; boyo, you should hear him curse. Compared to us, to our "sensibilities"—swill in a pail—this was old Greek wine, tasting of pitch and icy sea water. The day of his birth, day of conception, animals, plants, stones underfoot; sons and daughters (existent or no), camels, herds, sheep (ditto), the litany was a cosmic round. God could take it all, shove it up the blind bung hole of hell. He'd had it.

Until another mood set in, the chaos faded awhile. He moved like a wraith around his fusty dimmed out rooms, bathrobe and slippers, a ghost of a ghost, padded upstairs, there to commence according to my patient limits, some hours of sublime, exasperating, faith filled, talk talk talk. It was an old world exercise in elevated loquacity, seldom heard on these shores.

And as I came to realize, another form of that game he was playing and playing out, to the bitter end. If he could talk, he was still alive; a light tongue was surrogate for (formerly alas) light feet. In the book under (remote) consideration, God uses Satan for hit man. And who set this one against old Demos and myself? And for what reason? A debate with the Almighty? It sure as hell is indicated. Meantime, patience.

Demos; beyond any doubt the most misfortunate being I have ever encountered. It came to me when I looked into the ruined face of the one who calls him fathah. Down with cancer, count nine, his whereabouts hidden from this fat bird of prey who wants him, dead or alive. Not fathah, but a ripoff. Such indignity is a death before death.

The old man literally has no choices left. Where can he go in this world?

A flaked out voluble undefeated dignity about him, skinny legs crossed, little boy's plaid on his legs, the interminable cigarette like Lady Liberty's lamp, never extinguished. Demos, Demos! I'd yell at the door. He'd embody in the musty gloom, the warehouse of a parlor; nine tenths dead, grey as ash. A bad day, shades down night all day, every day. Fruit and soup, fruit and soup, pablum for Job's gums.

Or he sat there in the hospital, at end of the shoddy corridor, in a patch of light, in the grey of Good Friday. Grey; eyes, skin, fingers, cigarette smoke, the voice of the dead. Nature was drawing its shades, he was smoking his guts, as usual; it curled from his ashen nostrils. The chemotherapy was working in him, he was benign with that awful level calm of the near dead.

The Patience of Job in Detroit, Michigan

Have you ever floated along in a stream as a child, eyes half in, half out of water, half in, half out of light? Two worlds you perceive, one afloat, eery indistinct, evanescent, the other hard and clear and infinitely beloved, the crawl space of the land animal.

He was between worlds. Jaunty almost, an air of benignity, eyes of water, elbow crooked, the eternal flame.

He knew, he knew that you knew, and were uneasy; something more, something less, but in any case, something other; he drank from that point where the water leaped up and claimed the land, where the animals went down in a deluge. He drank knowledge at that point, he breathed both water and air, transmogrifying before our eyes.

He could afford to be benign. It was all but over. Victim of the world's implacable course, he was a conqueror. No greater throne, the dung heap.

He would up the ante, and refurbish the image; *a ligno regnat Christus*. It was Good Friday . . .

The church should censor the bible out of existence. Then we could all arrive at a fine four square gentleman's agreement about the universe and one another, and put our necks meekly under the embroidered boot of the grand inquisitor, whose role in such a case would be secular, sensible and final.

It is this constant pollutive outbreak of sores and boils, the metaphors which are not to our peace, that tear us apart!

How could you sit there, being lectured to by a doctor of philosophy (major in dying) and not have Job or Christ or both, steadfastly there also, immobile, ikons of misery and eventuality, standing to right and left, the thieving martyrs of history that creep back and back and back, to attend the dying, to score with their great agate eyes our trashy existence—score it with meaning, substance, accountability; beating a way through history's bloody smoke,

87

even as they snatch from the pit—ourselves, the skinny homunculi, racing to the edge, steeling for the dive, drunk with death, mad, hell gone for broke?

They stood there, right and left. They gave him that ramrod dignity that cannot be pulverized, not by cancer, not by addicts in the house, not by thugs, not by life.

He revels in their presence. He knows who is there, he draws his ragged breath like a mandarin, his head tosses balkily, sick and starved, all but transparent, a grave heavy with Easter seeds . . .

In the city of used cars and misused people. In the city where everything, toe to eye, is assailed and invaded with blear, with bad breath, with miles of flattened burnt out lives and dwellings.

In the city of regnant death. In the city of Good Friday where the cross looms high as Cleopatra's Needle.

And is raised and balanced there, by every cunning, every skill, every doom. In the city of human blur and soulless motion, where the rich live Grossly at the Point and the poor die and kill, mutual hunters and victims.

In the city which is furnace and laboratory of the inhuman future of all.

In the city which is primal image and earth mover and tank and motor—of all cities, a Nineveh, a Sidon, an Athens —and more.

In a city which observes like an uneasy ceasefire, a two day moratorium on murder (the first such space without bloodshed in anyone's memory).

In the city whose lovely trees coexist uneasily, turning on us in spring the eye of a fawn under the hunter's glare.

An eye of alarm, a doom.

In the city one generation advanced, even beyond America, in the art of self-destruction.

In the city which casts up day after day, from stacks and

assembly lines and car lots, from unutterable squalor, music and art and poetry.

In the city which issues day after day a somber state of the union message, a sinister state of the world message.

In the city which is a perpetual count down, down, down, on our crimes, on our chances . . .

Job of Detroit, pray for us.

Moses in Egypt:
A Diary of Exile

Such disarray! The first tentative step out of our morass was castigated; utopian!

The cry went up against the most innocent finger, following the most ingenuous blue eye in the world as it pointed say, to an infernal mushroom on the horizon; apocalyptic!

You were supposed to stand there.

You were supposed to give it all up, without a cry.

The whole country was like an enormous bathysphere; it sank 5 or 6 feet a year into the sea.

It was all so gradual, the wisest heads would turn in a fury if anyone from a marmoset to a child to a shaman dared say aloud, "look, we're sinking!"

We weren't supposed to sink; we couldn't be.

Apostles of normalcy went around campuses, churches, factories, lawcourts, stadiums, shaking timbrels, giving away knickknacks, buttons (I love me, whee!), candy, aphrodisiacs, flowers, messages from the beyond.

Some people began to itch like hell. But there was always a new foot powder or armpit spray.

Some people had trouble breathing. Mysterious inflamations crept into eyes, ears, throats, a confounded misery. The victims were told; Neuresthenic organic genital suppression. Get hold of yourself.

The state grew bold. Formerly it let its disasters trickle out to the public like water from a common spout. Now it dumped bad news on us like an avalanche, predicted more, reproved and threatened people.

They ordered all the clocks destroyed and gave out the time wrong. The same with the weather; they smashed barometers, seeded clouds and set a miserable rain, brown to grey to dirty green, falling on us.

Those days too, officials got aroused for another reason. Someone pointed out that their monuments were generally bigger than they were.

So the Top Leader ordered a twelve-foot image of himself made, face, limbs, uniform; it was hollow, filled out with a mechanism that looked like the cabin of a crane. He climbed up there and sat down at the controls, moving his arms and legs along the streets like an iron insect, announcing the weather and time of day into the microphone, all wrong.

That way he reached millions, from six feet above them.

The mask and clothing of the contraption could, of course, be altered. So Our Leader developed a favorite guise. It was a subtle mix of space man and bishop; inspired by certain classified triumphs in outer space and Sunday morning services in the White House.

He'd come on, cased in aluminum, arms and legs stalking along, with a great purple sheath over all. It was superb; he'd started something.

The others, cabinet members, congressmen, supreme court judges, followed in procession, carrying his train. They had copied his costume and moved about inside similar paraphenalia, only smaller.

It looked like a religious procession on the moon. You felt like laughing, you didn't dare cry.

You might think; at least I'm free to think in my head; what a lousy gang, pimps, crooks, liars. But the trouble was, if you had thoughts like that, they knew it, they could read you like a billboard. Or they thought they could, and it came to the same thing. You were jailed for intent.

So most people kept their mouths clean as their minds, and their minds clean as a funeral wreath. They hid out, quiet, under the wreath. RIP became a life slogan for many.

Those days if a pollster asked you in the street, "How do you feel about the result of the recent election? Great? Greater? Greatest?" you were advised to hitch up your shoulders and say loudly: "The greatest! What a greatest team we have!"

There was hardly a way left of signaling, even to yourself, left alone of saying to him: "back off, creep. A horse just kicked me."

Winners/Losers Or
Whose God is for Real

Ahab called all Israel together and assembled the prophets
on Mount Carmel. Elijah stepped out in front of all the
people. "How long," he said, "do you mean to hobble first
on one leg then on the other? If Yahweh is God, follow
him; if Baal, follow him." But the people never said a
word. Elijah then said to them, "I, I alone, am left as a
prophet of Yahweh, while the prophets of Baal are four
hundred and fifty. Let two bulls be given us; let them
choose one for themselves, dismember it and lay it on the
wood, but not set fire to it. I in turn will prepare the other
bull, but not set fire to it. You must call on the name of
your god, and I shall call on the name of mine; the god
who answers with fire, is God indeed." The people all
answered, "Agreed!" Elijah then said to the prophets of
Baal, "Choose one bull and begin, for there are more of
you. Call on the name of your god but light no fire." They
took the bull and prepared it, and from morning to midday
they called on the name of Baal. "O Baal, answer us!" they
cried, but there was no voice, no answer, as they
performed their hobbling dance around the altar they had
made. Midday came, and Elijah mocked them. "Call
louder," he said, "for he is a god: he is preoccupied or he
is busy, or he has gone on a journey; perhaps he is asleep
and will wake up." So they shouted louder and gashed
themselves, as their custom was, with swords and spears
until the blood flowed down them. Midday passed, and
they ranted on until the time the offering is presented; but
there was no voice, no answer, no attention given to them.
    Then Elijah said to all the people, "Come closer to me,"

and all the people came closer to him. He repaired the
altar of Yahweh which had been broken down. Elijah took
twelve stones, corresponding to the number of the tribes of
the sons of Jacob, to whom the word of Yahweh had come,
"Israel shall be your name," and built an altar in the name
of Yahweh. Around the altar he dug a trench of a size to
hold two measures of seed. He then arranged the wood,
dismembered the bull, and laid it on the wood. Then he
said, "Fill four jars with water and pour it on the holocaust
and on the wood"; this they did. He said, "Do it a second
time"; they did it a second time. He said, "Do it a third
time"; they did it a third time. The water flowed around
the altar and the trench itself was full of water. At the time
when the offering is presented, Elijah the prophet stepped
forward. "Yahweh, God of Abraham, Isaac and Israel," he
said, "let them know today that you are God in Israel, and
that I am your servant, that I have done all these things at
your command. Answer me, Yahweh, answer me, so that
this people may know that you, Yahweh, are God and are
winning back their hearts."

Then the fire of Yahweh fell and consumed the
holocaust and wood and licked up the water in the trench.
When all the people saw this they fell on their faces.
"Yahweh is God," they cried, "Yahweh is God." Elijah
said, "Seize the prophets of Baal: do not let them escape."
They seized them, and Elijah took them down to the wadi
Kishon, and he slaughtered them there. (1 Kings,
18:20–40)

There was this uncertainty, from the beginning; which
didn't improve as time went on.

Those who dared form the question didn't do so in public. Like Job they whispered it, usually to their armpit, curse
the day I was born. That was a challenge, more than normal.
But he went ahead with the script anyway, which was more
than duly harsh, a hint to those who could catch it—not just
Job, but us as well.

Still I was thinking of an earlier time. Maybe the reasoning had gone like this:

96

1) Let's show we're on the winning side. Then, when that's clear

2) Let's change sides. Join the losers.

I don't know how else to make sense of it. He certainly wasn't a loser at the start, he just as certainly wasn't a winner toward the middle. What the end will show—we're sweating through at the present.

To speak of the earlier time, from almost any point of view, the prophet made a most unsatisfactory showing with Baal.

What about those priests, sweating, grimacing, gyrating, all day, under the taunts of Elias? So your God's not showing up; be patient, boys, maybe he's gone to the outhouse; (literally) keep your spirits up, he'll be back!

And then finally under the Swath, the raised and lowered arm of Eliseus, that great vulgar whoooosshhh of fire, up and down like a mad Semaphore, which the Baalites couldn't kindle for the soul of them, which the prophet summoned, an instant fungus over the water-soaked logs, easily, against nature's usage, beyond the gaping jaws of the crowd. Not our favorite scene. Now he's made his point, and maybe he'll go quietly away.

It's a scene that raises at least as many questions as it answers. Like, what about those suddenly adoring multitudes? Where would they have gone, in what direction, supposing Baal had won? And what kind of faith is it that depends on a show of force so silly, arbitrary, humiliating to the loser? And what sublime and elevated soul first proposed the tourney, and then in all seriousness carried it off?

We must be missing something.

I would like a few things explained.

When things get difficult for our God (who is an embarrassing presence in his own bible, his own world) we like to pass things off with an airy reference to this or that recondite literary form. The equivalent of saying: he didn't mean it (supposing he did it); or a barefaced denial, he didn't do that; or (here comes the skeleton on roller skates); anthropologically speaking, why, we've been imputing our conduct to him, concocting a god in our own image. How gauche.

Then when things go well, so to speak, scripturally or in current life, we congratulate ourselves on a sound cosmic sense, superior sanitation, our native calling to greatness. We whip ourselves onward and upward; another war against another foe, yet another frontier to cross. In any case, a slogan to meet the emergency, a myth or a mace, or both.

When on the other hand, things go ill in current affairs (that is to say, almost always), there's always a God around to beat on. Such occasions make the advantages of theism apparent; great, someone exists, someone to blame. Thus, national distress is rendered bearable, and gross sin is subject to the intelligence of practicing Christians.

Anyway you will recall; at someone's suggestion, the prophet went ahead with the contest, evidently following on an agreement with the priests of Baal. And God won. Which, in the light of later developments, seems merely a preliminary to true religion, an introduction to the Christian treatment of adversaries.

Who are those gods anyway, who in our scriptures, are losers; and in other scriptures, are winners?

I would like to know more of them, on the supposition that they exist too, and when they flee a field of contest for a day or an eon, are not thereby disposed of. Perhaps in imitation of Jawe on *his* bad days, go underground, so to speak. And appear again in other guises, under other skies.

What I like in these otherwise gruesome contesting pages is the dramatic view of faith. Not an assent to propositions which promptly agreed to, are promptly forgotten.

But something gamey, up close, fearsome, like you cart

out your paraphenalia, I'll bring out mine; priesthood, dance, sweatbox, timbrils, incantations, favorite positions, potions, chants, imprecations, petitions, all of it. Name your gods. Challenge me to name mine. And let us, in rigorous contestation, see who comes through.

This, in crude outline, is a way of belief that is long gone, having at length "civilized" itself.

By no means. The same events still transpire, as I would argue. With the reservation noted above; the test of allegiance is no longer to be thought of (as indeed I would be hesitant to declare it was then thought of) as a vulgar pyrotechnic.

There were in fact, in those days as well as our own, other occasions and temptations, when the prophet of the true God lost—everything. And still stood firm. For which we honor him, and follow his God, a rag tag, a remnant, a people whose god's existence, like our own, runs so close to extinction that we cannot at times be sure he is there at all. At times? At most times, almost always.

Thus the contest with Baal is more in the nature of a running marathon than a single event. It is the way history goes; now this way, now that. Now in Baal's favor, now in God's. Neither side finally yielding the world to the other, neither at any time wholly done in.

How about this for a change? What seems to be God's foolishness is wiser than men's wisdom, and what seems to be God's weakness is stronger than men's strength. . . . Few of you wise or powerful or of high social standing, from the human point of view. God purposely chose what the world considers nonsense in order to put wise men to shame; and what the world considers weak in order to put the powerful to shame. He chose what the world looks down on and despises and thinks is nothing, in order to destroy what the world thinks is important. This means that no one can boast in God's presence. But God had brought you into union with Christ Jesus, and God has made Christ to be our wisdom; by him we are put right with God, we become God's holy people and are set free. So then as the scripture says, whoever wants to boast must boast of what the Lord has done.

The Tenth Generation According to Daniel

We dislike philosophical essays as much as the next one. Life has forced us, in the old language, to be undogmatic, mercilessly so. And everyone from rodents shaking in their holes to birds falling out of the befouled air, knows why. Time is a luxury, space a tamed wilderness. We are, or our children shortly will be, members of that fateful tenth generation which from Late Bronze to Hiroshima, has tattooed in blood, a large X on the face of the wall.

It behooves us, though, to make an attempt to get at the sources of this trouble. And thereby, perhaps, to deflect our fate. And even, to put to an end the malign practice, now much in vogue, of inflicting our fate beforehand on the provinces, Vietnam or elsewhere.

To begin then. Every people that bent its effort to create the Tenth Generation elsewhere, has also been marked by a pervasive religious spirit. It goes without saying. And I make little of the counter argument of the Marxists; they did away with God, but without notable improvement in the human condition, if we can judge the Russian instance. Russia is a fascist cauldron, as Solzhenitsyn has demonstrated (as well as other heroes, silenced, degraded, subjected to medical experiment, murdered, driven into exile). Roughly the same path was staked out by Hitler; wipe out the gods, who in the Protestant sense or the Orthodox sense, are strictly unmanageable, politically embarrassing.

Paradise, self-defined and created, will follow.

By one means or another, people have to be roused up, persuaded of their unique character, their being "chosen" for great deeds, for conquest and control of others. It all starts virtuously; in the bible, under the seal of a divine message, granted as predeliction to one tribe only. Thus the people are welded together, given a sense of being in the world, a common memory, a pride of place. All to the good, so far.

Where and how, and what the forces are that gather and explode, where an original promise and agreement gets bowlderized, deflected, bought—this remains a mystery. As mysterious, in fact, as the original happening; apparently so pure, so transcendent, so untouchable. History is a dirty rag, indeed, on the loins of Original Justice. This is acknowledged; but a question arises; what happened to Original Justice when the rag fell off?

From the point of view of consequence, there are no more perilous, incendiary words in all history, than the simple "I choose you" of the divine.

History is a slowly corrupting marriage, after a brilliant wedding day. The statement as offered is neither naive nor cynical, neither an attack on the innocence of the bride nor the integrity of the groom. But what has life itself done, to all that promise? We are appalled.

An original agreement was reached. In the case of Moses, it was sealed in blood, in a ceremony that was at once primitive, powerfully orchestrated in summons and response, at once appealing to and transcending the blood call. "Do you choose Jawe for your god? Then know that he has first taken you, Israel, for his people."

The effect of this can only be imagined. The people are bonded to God, to one another, in a way that only such a

102

scene can realize. They have entered on an adventure that will bring them time and again to the edge of glory, to the edge of extinction. And they will never be toppled. Never quite. It will bring them also in other directions, devious ones, the inventions of the secularist demons in their midst, and of the jackals and camp followers who feed off rotten marrow.

Thus we come to the present horror, which, if it could only be treated as parable or fable, would be laughable in the extreme. But as a matter of cruel and present fact, it summons only tears—for the living and the dead.

The fact being simply that the covenant has reached its dead end, its Tenth Generation. In a nation state like all the rest.

And we (as once they were) are bereft of alternatives. Of which they were the unique hope.

I remember Jeremiah. O betrayers of my people. . . . Have all but forgotten in the midst of the above threnody, to introduce myself. Daniel. A captive Jew, in a foreign court. Skilled at necromancy, a chancy talent, indeed, which lands me everything—from a share of the purple to a most discomfiting sound, at source; the grinders of beats.

I subsist somewhere in the middle; by that species of faith which is also a skill, God both conferring and conniving thereto.

Those who deal in dreams are in danger of themselves being consumed by their dreams. This judgment is cold fact, cold turkey. I have been through all that.

Have dealt with a stolid wall-eyed monarch, half mad with fear of his own smoky phantoms. Have dealt also with my own private hell. In the beginning, thought I need merely be clever, laugh up my sleeve, concoct a counter-madness to his. And so survive. But things were not that simple. The geometry of horror, in the case of dreams, is as inflexible as a configuration of stars; there is no escaping its metaphysic. And the longer I dealt in these matters, and the more renown I won, the more inflexibly I was drawn into the web; infinite spaces, fear of heights, the probability that I, too, would metamorphose into the beasts over which I claimed sovereignty. Necromancers, fakirs, wonder workers, mystics take warning.

We had to be more clever than our owners. It was not something native, to us, but in captivity we accumulated that stock of raw experience and finesse that would help us over red seas, deserts, promises that turned into slavery, slavery that opened doors. Sometimes, inevitably one languished in their jails, sometimes one crawled the earth, sometimes one lickspittled up to them. When they have you in their fist, when their lust shows in their bulging eyes, and you, you are the choicest morsel in sight; when the choices are so limited—why, you come up with something, a slice of wit, a sting, a mordant curse, a laugh even. Something that says, in whatever way is open to last ditch ingenuity: before I'm your morsel, I'm your fool. Have you ever once in your oafish existence, heard the truth? Listen to the fool.

What his besotted nattering star gazers couldn't know; the dreams of the mighty always follow a pattern. Dreams are invariably the unacknowledged underside of the anatomy of power, the part labeled obscene by the waking and watchful. That's a supposition you can know nothing of, until you've been there, until you're a permanent fixture of the tenth generation.

Architecture used to make plain what I speak of. The place was next door to the dungeons; in Venice, the two were joined by a stone bridge. The great hall, the sublime celestial regions of Tinteretto, demanded those "dark declivities" of the palace anatomy, the torture halls, the detention centers.

It was only in dreams that the body could be made whole, could walk as one, could stretch its thighs up and down the

104

stairs, in darkness, naked, visible to itself, purposeful, revealed, an epiphany of ravening desire, self-haunted, self-conscious at last. Glory cast aside, chains on ankles; broken. And alone, alone, only in dreams could he be alone, freed from his sycophants, his star watchers, his women.

The king said to Daniel (who had been given the name Belteshazzar), "Can you tell me what my dream was, and what it means?" Facing the king, Daniel replied, "None of the sages, enchanters, magicians or wizards has been able to tell the king the truth of the mystery which the king propounded; but there is a God in heaven who reveals mysteries, and who has shown King Nebuchadnezzar what is to take place in the days to come. These, then, are the dream and the visions that passed through your head as you lay in bed:

"O king, on your bed your thoughts turned to what would happen in the future, and the Revealer of Mysteries disclosed to you what is to take place. This mystery has been revealed to me, not that I am wiser than any other man, but for this sole purpose: that the king should learn what it means, and that you should understand your inmost thoughts.

"You have had a vision, O king; this is what you saw: a statue, a great statue of extreme brightness, stood before you, terrible to see. The head of this statue was of fine gold, its chest and arms were of silver, its belly and thighs of bronze, its legs of iron, its feet part iron, part earthenware. While you were gazing, a stone broke away, untouched by any hand, and struck the statue, struck its feet of iron and earthenware and shattered them. And then, iron and earthenware, bronze, silver, gold all broke into small pieces as fine as chaff on the threshing floor in summer. The wind blew them away, leaving not a trace behind. And the stone that had struck the statue grew into a great mountain, filling the whole earth. This was the dream; now we will explain to the king what it means. You, O king, king of kings, to whom the God of heaven has given sovereignty, power, strength and glory—the sons of men, the beasts of the field, the birds of heaven,

wherever they live, he has entrusted to your rule, making
you king of them all—you are the golden head. And after
you another kingdom will rise, not so great as you, and
then a third, of bronze, which will rule the whole world.
There will be a fourth kingdom, hard as iron, as iron that
shatters and crushes all. Like iron that breaks everything to
pieces, it will crush and break all the earlier kingdoms. The
feet you saw, part earthenware, part iron, are a kingdom
which will be split in two, but which will retain something
of the strength of iron, just as you saw the iron and the
clay of the earthenware mixed together. The feet were part
iron, part earthenware: the kingdom will be partly strong
and partly weak. And just as you saw iron and the clay of
the earthernware mixed together, so the two will be mixed
together in the seed of man; but they will not hold
together any more than iron will blend with earthenware.
In the time of these kings the God, of heaven will set up a
kingdom which shall never be destroyed, and this kingdom
will not pass into the hands of another race: it will shatter
and absorb all the previous kingdoms, and itself last for
ever—just as you saw the stone untouched by hand break
from the mountain and shatter iron, bronze, earthenware,
silver and gold. The great God has shown the king what is
to take place. The dream is true, the interpretation exact."
(Daniel, 2:26–45)

I knew the dream that had him transfixed, turned him to
ice. I knew it before he refused (or was incapable) of telling
it. "Tell me my dream," he blared like a stuck bull; not "In-
terpret my dream which I will proceed to recount to you,"
but "Tell me my dream, and then tell me its meaning."

His wise men were piddling on the marble flooring by
then, their knees knocking in their pantaloons. "Tell me my
dream!" He might as well ask them to transport his kingdom on a flying carpet. How could he demand the impossible? They were too close to power to smell its carrion soul.
He was asking the impossible because he had given up on
the possible. He was issuing orders from a throne in hell.
They smelled it and quaked.

I did too, and smiled. I took a look at him, a long look.
Stupid? Intelligent? Such qualities are beside the present
issue. He's at rope's end, that's the nub of the matter. He
hadn't slept, he was flayed alive by nightmares, midnight
stalkers, demons; by his soul imprisoned in its foul grandeur, its pigsty named Versailles. He was capable of only
one dream. I would tell it to him.

He had forgotten his dream, blotted it out, out of sheer
terror. I began from that fact, which I read in his mad
heifer's eyes. I would construct a dream for him, a dream
whose verisimilitude was beyond doubt, the truth of
heaven. I would tell him the dream he must have dreamed;
because he was king; and I was a Jew—two facts which gave
me immediate entry to his skull. As the saint knows the map
of hell; or as Beelzebub would know heaven; by opposition,
by loss. As a Jew, a slave, knows the souls of the oppressor.

O king, this was your dream.

(I offer you a commentary on my text, so exact, so admi-
rably true; hangman's humor spoken by the hanged.)

It had to be about a statue. For he was, in his soul, inert,
a self-lover, an idolater at his own shrine. What other subject was there in the universe but—himself?

Begin at the head. Begin with himself, the self appointed,
the self lover, the source of thought and decision (there are
no thought and no decision; he's at the mercy of others, a
statue). But his emptiness is called fullness. His dim wits are
named godlike; king, behold yourself O self deceived, image at the mercy of image makers. Begin with that.

In your dream O king, you saw a statue, the head of the
statue was pure gold, its chest and arms were silver, its belly
and thighs bronze; the legs iron, its feet partly iron and
partly tile.

Correct, O Great One? You dream of yourself, night
after night, and the dreams are not reassuring? You are
your kingdom, your power and glory, down to the iron
mines, down to the clay pits.

And then it breaks up. You break up.

While you looked at the statue, a stone which was hewn from a mountain, with no hands' skill, struck its feet, breaking them in pieces. The iron, tile, bronze, silver and gold all crumbled at once, fine as chaff on the threshing floor in summer. And the wind blew them away without a trace.

But the stone that struck the statue became a great mountain and filled the whole earth. A Jew's revenge.

You see, we can tell them their dreams because we are free of their demons.

When did I Daniel last dream of a colossus named Daniel? Ha!

The difference between our dream and his! Vast, incalculable. If the difference is ever diminished, so are we. If the difference is lost, so are we.

And note, too, the dream of the colossal One, his mirror image, is all against nature.

No one's that big. In life, in art. What's too big, comes down. If they could only be modest! That however, is not the achievement of the colossi, in the nature of things. Modesty can only be learned in the hard school which they conduct, but never attend. We do. Tuition free.

The outcome is against nature, too. Which is to say, we are. We're their outcome, it's hard to believe it—their children, their opposites. In this way; if you want to bring down old Goliath, image of an image of an image, you get yourself a smooth pebble, warm it like a mothering god, and watch it grow. Not fast, there's time, there's time. But even the stones of the road grow, if one is patient. That after all is our history, we patiently wait for the stones to rise like loaves of bread.   •

Within nature, outside nature. There's no resolution of all that in our case. Just as one can't so much as speak of a "resolution" in him. There's nothing to resolve, he's pure brute, pure inanition, pure thing. He's thrown into the

108

world, a factitious chancy image of something that never was, fruit of fevers, rare foods, late hours, diseased dreams. He's been thrown into the world, by chance; thrown upright. Now he only needs to be thrown down. Where I come in.

He doesn't dream about himself. He doesn't dream about his people, about the poor, the outcasts, victims of his wars and alarms. He doesn't dream about anything real. He dreams about—power. Which is to say, the least real, the most surreal, insecure, flamboyant, blood ridden will o' the wisp. There are some things I can't tell him.

And even when he dreams about his kingdom, which is his ersatz soul, his excuse for a breath of spirit, his animating boiler—even then, he has trouble patching things together. It isn't a good arrangement, even by his standards. He knew it; his fingers are bitten to the quick.

Part of the genius of my dream (his dream) is this; I kept him top dog. In fact he's no more than a dead head on the end of a stock. Still, I made him of gold, the noblest roman of them all, the noblest metal, for capstone. That pleased him. He looked up from gnawing his moustache and actually smiled. It was like sunlight on a ruin.

Iconoclasts. Get them to lose confidence in their dreams. A religious exercise. No graven images. A small, even a slavish task. Termites. The long haul. The point at which this totally self-enclosed, brilliantly coped, doomed universe—needs me! A breakthrough. The stone that grows.

You must admit the last detail, the stone that grew to fill the whole earth, was a detail beyond all praise. Also a moment of considerable daring. I had to rely on my sense of him; completely devoid of malice, a pure, instinctive, single minded killer. A sense of irony isn't often a part of the imperial equipment. So I could stand there, in all seriousness, a short haired, wide eyed innocent out on bail, nothing to lose, nothing to gain, and actually predict his downfall, his utter ruin, the end of his world. And he, straining forward, strung out, verifying every detail, nodding his noodle like a metronome, as though his own ruin were the sweetest news in the universe. As though my dream were his middle name.

A Jew. Believes that pebbles grow into ostrich eggs, and hatch. Believes dreams are realer than daylight. Stretches the attention of tyrants like a band of rubber; and then, ping! Lets it go.

They're after your soul. So you go after theirs. It's a contest. You win because you have landmarks; that's precisely what they lack. So they think they have you; one day with honors and bullion and purple robes (all the bribes that bribe them); another with chains on your limbs. Turning eggs back to stone. They want to scramble you, extreme applications of hot and cold reality to sensitive parts. Torture and ecstasy. You have to have land marks.

He sat there for a long time after my exegesis was finished. The truth hurts, that was the chance I took. But the shoe also fits. He got up suddenly, and walked on it. I knew then that I had won—this round. He stood in the window with his back to me; ahead of him, vista on vista of splendid gardens, peopled by his statues of gold, bigger than life, lacquered from head to foot, naked as newborn gods. His dream, on pedestals. Himself, the imperial inflation, multiplied mile after mile. Broad daylight, and his delusions spread out before him, an animated tapestry. Himself, in mirrors. His life.

You try this, it doesn't work. So you try that. It doesn't work. That's being a Jew. Nothing works.

Being a king is not much different, everything seems to work. And it does work, for a time. For the space of a trumpet blast. Then you're an echo, too. Welcome O conqueror, to the losing side. Where theres's always room. Move over, worms.

110

The Book of Abdiah: A Commentary of Sorts

1. I have received a message from Yahweh,
   a herald has been sent throughout the nations,
   'Up! Let us march against this people.
   Into battle!'

2. The Lord Yahweh says this:
   Now I am going to reduce you among the nations,
   and make you utterly despised.

3. Your pride of heart has led you astray,
   you whose home is in the holes in the rocks,
   who make the heights your dwelling,
   who say in your heart,
   'Who will bring me down to the ground?'

4. Though you soared like the eagle,
   though you set your nest among the stars,
   I would fling you down again—it is Yahweh who speaks.

5. If robbers came to you,
   or plunderers at night,
   they would steal to their heart's content.
   If grape-gatherers came to you,
   they would leave no gleanings behind them.

6. How you have been pillaged!
   How Esau has been looted,
   his hidden treasures rifled!

7. They have driven you right to the frontiers,
   they have misled you, all your allies.

They have deceived you, your fine friends.
Those who ate your bread now set traps for you,
'He has no intelligence now.'

8. When that day comes—it is Yahweh who speaks—
shall I not deprive Edom of sages,
the Mount of Esau of intelligence?

9. Your warriors, Teman, will be seized with terror
until not a single one is left
in the Mount of Esau.

10. For the slaughter, for the violence
done to your brother Jacob,
shame will cover you
and you will vanish for ever.

11. On the day you stood by
as strangers carried off his riches,
as barbarians passed through his gate
and cast lots for Jerusalem,
you behaved like the rest of them.

12. Do not gloat over your brother
on the day of his misfortune.
Do not exult over the sons of Judah
on the day of their ruin.
Do not play the braggart
on the day of distress.

13. Do not pass through the gate of my people
on the day of its misfortune.
Do not, in your turn, gloat over its disaster
on the day of its misfortune.
Do not lay a finger on its treasures
on the day of its misfortune.

14. Do not take your stand at the crossroads
to cut off its fugitives.
Do not hand over its survivors
on the day of distress.

15. For the day of Yahweh is near
    for all the nations.
    As you have done, so will it be done to you:
    your deeds will recoil on your own head.

16. Yes, as you have drunk on my holy mountain,
    so will all the nations drink unsparingly;
    they will drink, and drink deep,
    and will be as if they had never been.

17. But on Mount Zion there will be some who have
    escaped
    —it shall become a holy place—
    and the House of Jacob will despoil
    its own despoilers.

18. The House of Jacob shall be a fire,
    the House of Joseph a flame
    the House of Esau a stubble.
    They will set it alight and burn it up,
    and no member of the House of Esau shall survive.
    Yahweh has spoken.

19. Men from the Negeb will occupy the Mount of Esau,
    men from the Lowlands the country of the Philistines;
    they will occupy the land of Ephraim and the land of
    Samaria,
    and Benjamin will occupy Gilead.

20. The exiles from his army, the sons of Israel,
    will occupy Canaan as far as Zarephath;
    and the exiles from Jerusalem now in Sepharad
    will occupy the towns of the Negeb.

21. Victorious, they will climb Mount Zion
    to judge the Mount of Esau,
    and the sovereignty shall belong to Yahweh.
                                        (Obadiah, vv. 1–21)

Chapter 1, verse 1. The Book of Abdiah is the shortest book of the Old Testament. It contains one chapter of twenty one verses.

C.1, V.2 This commentary will surpass Abdiah, it will contain one chapter of twenty verses.

1, 3. Thereby we will both set a record of sorts, and establish a good example for future prophets and commentators.

1, 4. The Book of Abdiah is about vengeance and violence.

1, 5. This in itself is hardly remarkable, since practically all old testament books contain elements of vengeance and violence.

1, 6. What makes this book unique, is short as it is, it is *all* and *only* about v. and v.

1, 7. This is just fine though because, as one commentator put it, the vengeance envisioned in the book is a *universal* violence, meted out by Jawe against *all* nations. That makes it just right.

1, 8. So no one who reads the Book of Abdiah (or for that matter, this unworthy commentary) in any language, in any skin, under any sky, is to be anything but comforted.

1, 9. Because as is clear from this book, Chicken Big is the enemy of everyone who is an enemy of anyone. That should be clear by now.

1, 10. If perchance this is still unclear, it's because you're 1) blind 2) deaf 3) dumb 4) retarded 5) non-Jewish 6) non-Christian 7) or all or some of the preceding.

1, 11. If you're only a common citizen almost anywhere in the world, you probably know much of the preceding anyway, without the Book of Abdiah.

1, 12. The knowledge that things are bad and

1, 13. getting worse is hidden away in no one's attic, nor is it lurking in someone's diplomatic pouch.

1. 14. Nor would it seem to require a divine revelation to bring the news home,

1, 15. (if by "home" is meant the generality of humans, widely dispersed as to language, color and ethnic background,

1, 16. sharing none the less one universal trait, a kind of birth-mark stamped early in our career, on our most public part, viz., our phiz).

114

1, 17. To wit, we are getting shafted. Universally. Responsibility for this fact of life is variously ascribed, according to one's language, color, ethnic background, to fate, providence, Jawe, Buddha, Krishna, Jesus.

1, 18. And their servants and emissaries, authorities and subalterns, to whose tender mercies Christians are commended in Romans, c. 13. But this is perhaps carrying our subject too far afield.

1, 19. If vv. 17–18 have left you severely depressed, may I suggest a contrary view, that of Revelations, c. 13, which depicts these same revered powers in a different light than the above cited texts; that is, as arrayed in a kind of omnibeast outfit, nightmarish and havoc making, murderous, duplicitous, etc., etc.

1, 20. So to conclude. You and I have a choice of sorts; on the one hand, a lineup of raw silk suits peddling hell under the brand name heaven; and on the other hand, the same hornrimmed brain trust, concealed in green mottled snake suits, making their way sinuously through your neighborhood, briefcases looped over their tails. This last verse is becoming quite lengthy; still, I cannot help advising that if your choice rests on the first of the above mentioned, you take a good look at the fine print on the contract; and if the second, that you run like hell.

A Brief Press Conference
with God on the Fate
of a Favorite Son

Reporter: "Will you comment please on Solomon, his immense earthshaking exploits, his temple and concubines, his terebinth, his wisdom and folly, the disposition he made of the perplexing case of the two mothers and the living and dead babies, his worshipfulness and his hardcore porno tendencies, his encouraging or at least countenancing of questionable rites in the notorious high places, his foreign wives, his alien gods, the bad ending he purportedly made?"

no comment saith the Lord

Reporter: "Have you seen him lately? Is he with you now?"

no comment saith

Jeremiah, or God is a Downer

What do you do when you can't live in peace?

I don't know. I do know that without inner peace, there is no peacemaking.

What do you do when you can't live virtuously?

I am reasonably sure that if one cannot live virtuously, and cannot even live with the thought that one cannot so live, one will be tempted by death—virtuously or not. And that is quite an illusion; name me a greater!

A sense of being in midstream, out of one's depth. And no landmarks—if by landmarks is meant some point in nature, some rock or tree, against which to measure; we are here, we have come so far.

Maybe human "marks"; but these are no marks at all, since we are all in the stream, all out of our depth, all being borne along. Thus it is cold comfort that some are with me, a semblance of being planted on terra firma (one grows skilled at vertical water treading); but the same look is in the eyes of all, or nearly all—out of my depth!

Thus "where are we?" is a variant on "who are we?"—a metaphysical crisis. Questions that should never arise, given a right sense of one's self, of one's task on earth, of creaturehood.

"I have seen the heavens open and I have seen the heav-

119

ens closed. And I am at a loss to say which is the greater terror."

It is only God who can tell us who He is.

A deceptively easy statement, smelling faintly of popular preachments. But I mean something serious. People are surreptitiously opening the bellies of chickens and consulting their entrails, scrutinizing the stars, ululating in chorus, making of God the excuse for everything from gun running to butter churning. He is as bent into the culture as they are, he is no more than the play of their wounded despairing frivolous consciousness. And, I almost forgot, of their suicide pacts. A prominent church pair does themselves in. Another theologian avers: they did right.

Which indeed they did; given despair, given faithlessness.

The demons would like to persuade us; we are the only ones who can tell you who we are. Untrue. Only God can tell us who the demons are. And he has named the father of the tribe Beelzebub, which is to say, father of lies. Thus naming the tribe and giving the lie to their lie.

You have heard the story of the man whose house is possessed by a demon. He is driven out, the house is cleansed, the man is at peace. And yet the demons are not amused, nor quelled. They say one to another, let's try again. And seven replace the one, and claim the lost ground —this time irrevocably, as it seems.

What went wrong? Perhaps exorcism is not enough.

Politically speaking, the liberal solution to a bad situation always is, "let's replace the incumbent." So creating a vacuum. Then the Blight House is an echoing invitation for seven demons to enter, to do seven times as much harm.

We are fated, it seems, to be "possessed"; in one sense or another, by one spirit or another. It is the very condition of creaturehood. The vacuum is also a violence.

120

Exorcism can be only the prelude to invitation. Begone Satan. Come Holy Spirit.

The king wants a prophet. I tell him to go buy himself one. Any one of a thousand can be bought for a song; overnight accommodations at the Big House will do. What he wants to buy is what they have to sell. What they have to sell usually goes like this: 1) Be assured that great is good. 2) Nothing ominous hangs over you; least of all judgment, least of all a sword. 3) What hangs over you, if the metaphor is a useful one (and to such a charlatan biblical images are only one choice among many) is the "shekinah"; favor, promise, more power. 4) And for the pressing of flesh, and for those arrangements which gentlemen never need to make explicit, our thanks, O Thou King of Clout!

He would like to have me, Jeremiah, killed, but the move is impolitic. There are other ways; he can negotiate my reduction to a non-person.

Hold up a broken vessel on a street corner, dejected. Or put a yoke on your shoulders like a beast of burden. Or dig in the earth until you touch damp earth. Then take up a handful, foul your countenance with it, eat it! They will shortly call you mad. Because you are miming, dramatizing their (and your) existence.

And this is not allowed. You have broken a taboo, which the myths have laid down, about God, about ourselves. "O fortunate people . . . It is both sweet and fitting to die for one's country . . . My country, right or wrong . . ."

Symptom of the time; no one listens.
Symptom; everyone talks.

What is the moral equivalent, in us, of Vietnam? Answer: everything, everything. Immobility, amnesia, moral blindness, the durability and saleability and persuasiveness and inner coherence of—violence. The moral equivalent of an exterminated people is the moral extermination of the aggressor. We who are powerless to change the facts, or deflect their outcome, can only mourn over the facts, and in minimal measure, expiate them.

"It is only the lowly, I thought, who are foolish; for they know not the way of the Lord, their duty to their God. I will go to the great ones and speak with them, for they know the way of the Lord, their duty to their God. But one and all, they had broken the yoke, torn off the harness."

Jeremiah, the real is so real I will die of it. Death at the hands of Jesus or the Buddha, their compassionate hands. The real is sur-real.

That was my crime. I told them of reality. And they killed me for it. I was supposed to bless their demons and call them angels, to shore up the myths, to give them a second life, another vindicating voice. To say peace peace, when there is no peace. But I said, no peace, there is no peace; when all their hounds of war were screaming as they laid waste, Peace, Peace!

It is a crime to be alive today. It is a crime to be out of prison. It is a crime to have a roof over one's head, it is a crime to have food on the table. It is an unimaginable crime to be honored, to travel freely, to step aboard aircraft, to pass money from hand to hand; every word is a criminal utterance.

It is by living that we enact again and again, the Original Crime. Expiation? A way out? Smile. I have overcome the world.

Learn to walk gracefully under a crushing weight, like

Obu women on their way to market. And what is more graceful than the long tailed fish, iridescent and supple as feathered peacocks, who move in the ocean depths? But where pressure is least, is a zero, no life at all is found. In outer space, only technological junk.

I wish it were possible to be born to something beside tragedy. But when, or where would that have been? Indeed in any age, innocence belongs to the dead and the newly born.

And what shall the rest of us do, in a world reduced to a set of whirling millstones, where we 1) grind the bones of others to make our bread, or 2) consent to be ground under?

They want heroes; but they want them for dinner. Hero sandwiches. And this is a very ancient story. Orpheus piped their tune, and they tore him to pieces. Martin King did not pipe their tune, and they slew him. Every one dies. The question is, what do we leave behind for others? A gun (the definitive solution, the silencer)—or a vision?

"The dreadful has already happened." Mr. Heidegger is, of course, correct; from the foundation of the world. The beast is in the sanctuary, in the holy of holies. Because we are there? But we are not bestial enough, not totally beast enough, to qualify. The abomination of desolation, the principalities and powers, the demons, Lucifer, Beelzebub, these beings come to the world, well heeled, well timed, well primed. And perhaps above all, "well-comed." God has named them; we ignore them at mortal risk.

You're helpless as a babe in a hurricane. Unless you want to carry a gun (against a hurricane?). Or enlist in violence (phone the cops!).

Call me Jeremiah.

The Fioretti
of Saint Eliseus˙

Believe me, I'm a once and only. Conceived by a miracle
in 4 Kings 4, 17, later died (lamented, indeed, but in the
course of nature) in 4 Kings 4, 20. And raised from the
dead (miracle again) in 4 Kings 4, 35.

With such a start, no wonder my life shows a wild mix
of colors, moods, outcomes.

But to begin where it began. My mother was old, my
father older. They had much wanted—not me, which
would be absurd, but some abstract and loveable entity,
forever perfect, just out of reach, weightless, ungoverned,
beyond discipline, diapers and night squalls—a child, any
child.

But no such thing arrived for years and years.

Then Eliseus, who used to come around invariably as the
new moon, came around again. He was a great man for
human misery. Since suffering was as impenetrable to him
as to anyone else, and since God vouchsafed little light to
him (as to why unwanted babies fell like hailstones in Janu-
ary, or why wanted ones were rare as lottery winners) since
all this was true, Eliseus had come on something commonly
referred to in charismatic circles as "another way."

Simply put, he was a cosmic repair man. Obviously, he
could do nothing about the wall the almighty had raised

between mere humans and right reason. He couldn't stop the hailstorm of unwanted souls falling to earth, breaking to pieces there; nor could he open the heavens and decree a rainfall of wanted infants, each one just right, blond or brunette, grey or blue or hazel of eye, falling straight on target into mother's arms.

Nor could he perform what to some heads might appear a lesser miracle. He couldn't even explain to us, ready enough as we were to credit a credible story—he couldn't tell us why on his favorite planet wrong was so bloody frequent and right so golden rare.

We didn't know; we still don't know, though he's long dead, and I as decrepid as he was once. We don't know; moreover, there's never been anyone, from the almighty down to the windfalling babies, who could explain any of these things to our satisfaction.

Hence, Eliseus, and his job—cosmic repair. Patch up, pick up, slap together, mend the roof and walls, plug the blind windows, keep the weather out and the people snug; that was his holiness. And say alleluia when you least feel like it, though it's said with a grim jaw and a breaking heart. That was his holiness too.

───────────────── 2 ─────────────────

Not like the rest of us, who shake our heads like bewildered animals in their rut and round, who lower our backs with half a will or no will at all, to what he's pleased to call *his* will (poverty, death, too many children, no children at all). Lower our heads for the next blow, mutter a prayer, wipe the tears from our eyes, and go on. Until death do us in.

We look to the heavens; no predicting the weather. We look to the earth, and slog on. We look at one another; world's end.

126

For some of us, that's life and death in a nut shell.

Then there are others. I call them the overwhelmed. They sit in church with the rest of us, they till the same fields and keep the same shops, they lie head to foot with us in graves. But there's such a difference among us as makes the stars sweat in their courses.

We don't give a damn, they say. Not a damn, big daddy. And the long and short of it and the height and depth of it and the come around and go around of it is—we don't give a damn because you don't. Tell us, how does it feel when the big yawn meets the little yawn? You know it; we've lost so much, even you don't seem too big a loss any more. Now I lay me down to sleep.

3

I Eliseus can't exactly say I'm on their side. I can't say I'm on anyone's, even his. Maybe it's because I'm a special case. How can you help but be wary when your life's a continuous tumbling about in the providential grab bag?

Consider my course; wanted, withheld, born out of time. (A perfect conjunction there; desire, intervention, joy, the flesh in all its glory.)

And then, blasted like a flower in a hailstorm. Born out of due time, perished out of due time. Tears again, a double loss.

4

When, indeed, will the sublime arbiter make up his mind, does he want me alive, does he want me dead? For look, a crowning miracle, one that sets the planets spinning, off their heads. I was dead, and I live. Sometimes I hold my hand before my face, trembling like a blade of grass, a blind man, sight restored, reading his palm, his fate.

It was a miracle that paled all the others, from the straight shadow I cast, up to his very throne, I am his miracle, a crowning miracle, a comeback momentous as Lazarus. A risen Jesus, exulting, exalted.

Why, when you think of it, I set Eliseus up in the world. The people would never again let him down, let him walk the earth like other mortals. He was raised to their shoulders, a sunrise, their host and cup at dawn. (And I gurgling and murmuring in my mother's arms, half articulate, self-delighted!)

We can't have it all, the world being what it is. You'd think, wouldn't you, if our heads were seamless as an egg, the universe would be that way too, without fault? You'd think so. You wouldn't think things would be continually falling to ground like a spilled and spoiled nest, nestlings scattered, dead and stinking?

---------- 5 ----------

But here we are, I've no need of reminding you. People with sound heads, looking for a world that makes sense, because that's what heads are made for, that's what the catechism tells them to expect. And they take their sound heads into the world and bam! The world makes as much sense as—no babies, dead babies, unwanted babies; all those tears, those prayers, those stopped grey lips, all that despair.

Then sometimes, the biggest bang of all, though there's a question whether the one it happens to ever gets to hear it. Anyway, the sensible egg splits, a yolk on a griddle. He's had it for this world; a few prayers, a few tears, he's shoveled under with the rest.

---------- 6 ----------

But there has to be more. Because otherwise you see, we'd all go crazy instead of dying Christian deaths. There

128

has to be more, some distance, some breathing space. Between the crack of doom and the doom sayer. Between the sound heads, yours and mine, that walk around as though we swam in a sound universe. Between the sanity packed into the skull, everything needed for the long march—and the insanity turning the big wheels. So we hang on to sanity —by the nerve of a tooth.

We're not supposed to die insane! That cry is our salvation. All this being so, enter the Holy Man.

A bloody job, at best. Eliseus had to walk in professionally, so to speak, and bring things together, draw some sense out of it all. And do this moreover, not in some remote shady grove, out of sight and sound of the mad world.

But in the very breach, the clout of it. In the crotch, where babies are made and not made. Where they're crushed, suffocated, stillborn, where their heads pop out and their eyes open, and they meet a welcome or a curse. Where the pleasure resides, too; where the joy stick enters into joy, big with resolve and blind as wood. The twilit thicket of Dante, death in a savage paw.

——————— 7 ———————

Enter the Holy Man. He's born, anointed, blessed, pushed forward. For one thing, one thing only. He's to make sense of the senseless world; blind, voracious, foul as pitch; a grave, a birth place. He's a baby maker, he leases life out. He's like a god, only better. He repairs the botched work, saves the repute of a bad workman.

That is to say, after all is said and done, and all preliminaries are over, he's in charge of the gates of creation. He lets some babies through, they get born. He holds others back, unwanted. In such a way, by such skilled coverups and unsearchable transactions, he keeps us from making up our minds. He keeps us on edge, unwillingly sane, unwillingly religious. What might be called unhopefully hopeful. Not quite stone blind. Not quite despairing.

While he's around, I've an excuse for saying, in some remote parochial turf, before the world's been allowed in, and the atmosphere has all the spurious cheer of a Sunday school in the suburbs, "things are not all that bad." Or in the accents of the latest bloated expert to win a grant from the Big One to apprehend our fate, "Studies only go to show."

In any case, and summing things up, "the evidence is not all in." We're taught to say it, early and late, the cry is nicked into our tombstones; the evidence is not all in.

——————————— 8 ———————————

Just as though the world were a zero, and the passing show a zero, and the faces we meet on the street, and the lives that sink to knee around us and fall without a cry. The evidence is not all in. As though the evidence could ever be in. Not all are born yet, not all have died; not all are in torment, not all are happy. Not all believe, not all curse and cry out—not all are in—in the sheepfold, in the grave.

Some evidence is in though. My credentials are in. Everything I have to go on.

Everything anyone has to go on? Maybe—I can speak only for myself. For I'm the work not only of a father and mother; there was the Holy Man, too. A trinity made me. So I know a few things—beyond most.

——————————— 9 ———————————

Something more. No one invited me to get born. Quite the contrary. First they said, no thank you. No child. Then they got fervent in the other direction, they wanted me like pearls, like—well they couldn't quite get it out, they could

130

only sit and pant and dream. Then they stood up and said, come along you, today. That kind of treatment gives you two tongues and four eyes.

It also gives you a divided mind.

Somewhere between prayer and despair. That's where I wander or would wander, if that third thing hadn't happened.

Please bear with my sense of being a special case. It isn't by way of pride I assure you. Sometimes, I think, if I could only weep. That would at least put me to one side or the other, tears for prayer, tears for despair. As it is, look at me. Look and run.

Anyway, I was born, a common enough occurance. To the flagrant joy of both parties, old parties not much used to joy. I can still see those rheumy eyes of my mother, they gathered all their blue, their clarity and focus, whenever she so much as recalled that day. Her eyes were grey, grey, to match her hair. But from the day I was born they weren't grey at all, they were blue as noon skies.

And her withered arms, what strength they held, like springs cleared, uplifted, welling. Her bones grew young, she danced about with me. I was her joy. She sang. She was a maid again, that old quavering voice cleared like a well's echo. My darling, my darling, she blushed and paled in the singing; ecstasy, too poignant a belief, almost a disbelief. I was born, I was in her arms!

So there we were, three of us, in that little enclosure, out of the world and time. Where things made sense. Where the sense came through, a miraculous childbirth. Where making sense meant making love, making a baby in their old bodies. It was more than sense, it was ecstasy.

Still, in their wild transport, they forgot something. They forgot the universe, in whose coils they rested—snug, mortally unsafe. They were drunk with life, they forgot death.

131

10

Then one day, the universe gave them a nudge. The coils closed. It was that simple. It's always a fairly simple project to destroy a life—or a million lives. Here the purpose was a fairly modest one; destroy this family.

It took no more than the tic of a dragon in its sleep; a shudder, and the beast slept again. We who were loving and joyous and sufficient to ourselves, were no more than the flash of a bad dream to him. But it was enough.

I died, that was all. In my mother's arms, where I lay night and day, to her joy and my bawling satisfaction. Red rose one day, white death another. Joy, life, birth; those were the illusions, the moon phases. The cottage and everyone in it, belonged to Big Boot, the interloper. He'd come hunting.

She sat there, a caricature of a mother. A shell of a woman, with the shell of a child in her bosom. Grief beyond grief, senselessness; the real world.

Afield, my father sensed something wrong, threw down his tool and came running. He'd caught something, a stink of plague, on the prevailing wind. Prevailing disappointment, prevailing death. His tears started before he even threw the door open, or saw her sitting there, her head riding in a fever of grief, the tears raining down. Then they were back at their lifetime occupation, comforting one another, broken, cheated, tears, prevailing tears, the common unction and lubricant of life.

Well, I remember something of that death.

If it seemed like a brutal kidnapping, I had to infer that part later. Whoever seized me, did it gently; death was no Herod. It was more like this; someone taking me up ever so gently from the arms of a sleeping woman. So gently! Only a stirring in sleep; no grief, a slight shift, a hand under me, warmth to warmth.

And then a chill, the door opened. The cold of the world
blew in.

_____ **11** _____

I awakened somewhere in a meadow, sat up.
Flowers around
the only light of that place
a multitude of flowers, a stillness so deep,
the stillness a world of its own
a length of luminous string
lying there in the grass and flowers
picked it up where it lay
and walked, it slipped through my hands,
length on length
unrolling perhaps from a spool out of sight
as one flies a kite
or fishes with an outgoing current
long long long
and all alight,
and I knew,
though I cannot tell how I knew,
I was to walk and hold the string,
whatever space would be required,
whatever direction
mildly curious I went,
a child,
freed from suffering, fever, fretfulness,
walked a certain space not easily measured
then gradually
something of cold, succeeding warmth,
day growing cold
the light of flowers
fading also,
the string cold wet to touch,

as though it were drawn, not from warm earth,
but from freezing hands
cold, body cold,
then loneliness, darkness,
touched suddenly the end of the icy string,
fell with a cry,
the bitterness of what is named
before it is tasted, death.
Then another wonder!
Before harm or blow befell,
taken up again,
in warm arms, and there wakened.

————————— 12 —————————

No I want to modify that last line, the slip of an old man's memory.

The first place I remember was my own bed, upstairs in the house: the first person I remember was Eliseus. The weight of his body on mine, suffocation. He was giving me my life back, mouth to mouth. My life back, out of his. That was the anomaly; no longer the world's breath I was sucking in, neutral air. It was his, I was living off his soul. And so perilously near the soul of the almighty one, that celestial bellows, that giver of life and taker of life, the one that sent me racketing on these mad journeys, that prevailer blowing me along on all winds, unwanted, wanted, unborn, born, safe born, dead. And now back from the dead. And from that day, how could such a one as I hope to be left alone, to undergo the "ordinary course of things" which I saw others undergo—born, washed, nursed, grown like a squash, dead like a stone?

This second birth, a kind of slice out of a prophetic pie. I was cursed, so to speak, with a blessing. Too much beholden, therefore, too, selfish. Knowing too much, therefore, doubly ignorant. Loving too much, therefore doubly bitter. Given too much, too many miracles, therefore spoiled. A painted child on a painted horse. Model of what? I was forbidden to ask. You know the way of them; some things keep happening only if they're ignored—while they're happening. The elders were all suavity and sadness and wisdom, conspirators at the sweetest game conceivable —to nail me to the wall.

Finger in the air, finger to lips, they warned and warned, a forest of stormy heads, and those severe loving pursed looks that drive a child mad with the assumption of superior wisdom. I must be taught it. I was never to forget it. I was subject and predicate and object and modifier of their love (they said), of their hunger (in fact), hanging there in the void by a thread, the thread of a miracle. Child, be grateful, be humble, be good. Or else!

Now between dying once, and dying twice, there may be much time, or little.

But much or little, there is no great choice concerning the future.

I could stew over those memories, reverting like a snail to its shell, for cover, for protection, for echo.

———————————— 13 ————————————

But Eliseus fascinated me. He took such brutal voltage from on high, and survived. Not only that, he and I were joined by the strangest bond in creation. Who had ever owed what I owed to mortal man? I looked again and again at the outstretched palms of my hand, their cunning tegument; and couldn't decide whether he deserved their blessing or their grip around his skinny throat.

Don't owe too much.

I owed too much. I became his disciple.

14

There was the matter of the ax head, the matter of sour waters, and the matter of the earth gone sterile. Also the matter of the hunger of the multitude, and their thirst. And innumerable matters of war and policy. He had his nose in everything; his eyes missed no more of the world than the sun does on the brightest days. A man would have had to build a thick hut, blackest pitch and thatch, no windows, and hide himself in it, to escape this pair of cormorant eyes.

It became clear to me in time; he had no less a project in mind, than the remaking of the world.

And then with more time, something became clear to me, that the earlier judgment stemmed from my own immodesty, my own inflated five year plan for retooling heaven and earth, my own hatred at the slow stalling nag named time. No, he was after something else. He went about the earth with no more cover than a wild animal, leaving a spoor for the other wild ones, who might or might not sniff it and read its message right.

I would, in time. The clues were unmistakeable. They said, not yet. They also said, almost. And, laugh with me, weep with me. And again, look around you; for the tiniest circle of things renewed, is the vast round of the universe, renewed. Also, be patient. Which is to say, be impatient.

Nothing was too big for him to tackle, nothing too small. We had gone one day to the bank of the Jordan. (He attracted disciples like Franciscans flocking to a revival.) So went cutting wood, to build a lean-to on the lean-to that passed for our shelter.

I was almost merry, to a fault. There were fifty of us; most were too young to know the world, or to renounce it; many would move on south, like the birds of Francis, if winds turned shrewd.

But could they sing! It was enough to make one forget

136

the winter coming on, the winter so hardly past. And the sun, and the delicious delicate air, entering every crevice of my hidebound mind like a wine, like a balm. Breathing that air, I almost forgot that unlike the flock around me, I had never been young, and would shortly be old.

I forgot it for an hour; when they had been young, I had already been dead. That when I was restored to life, the youth was wrung out of me.

But here I was, singing with the rest of them; so near to joy, and yet so distrustful of it, as to admit myself only to its outer edges. Go gingerly friend, eggshells underfoot!

Yet in my frosty distrusting way, rejoicing too, in their warmth, in their joy. Holding my hands to the warmth of life, for a few hours at least.

Under our urging, Eliseus had come with us to the river. So the day turned into a kind of picnic. Plenty of work, bringing down the trees in that lovely whispering grove by the Jordan, pausing for lunch together, the repartee and nonsense, all of us lightminded as pollen. In the late afternoon we set to work again, cleaning up, hauling the logs out.

Then a cry went up at the river.

As it happened, nothing worth turning a hair about. An ax head had gone flying off its handle midway in someone's particular lusty stroke. The iron landed splashing, somewhere out in midstream. That was all.

But the young monk was rueful, sorrowful. He'd borrowed the blade from a shepherd, and now it was gone beyond retrieving.

But Eliseus was as concerned as though a baby had been tossed away, and was lost out there, drawing a last watery breath. He asked, where do you judge the iron fell?

His eyes were scanning the ground as he spoke. He stooped and picked up a large flat wedge of wood; and when someone pointed directly out (second guessing I'd say) Eliseus spun the shingle out over the stream, where it fell and sank with a splash.

And then it surfaced again, under a hundred gaping eyes and fifty saucer mouths; there was the ax blade riding the shingle, riding it, not with the current which was in flood, but riding the waters ashore, as though spooled in by those grey eyes of his: inshore the cargo came, meek as a trained animal answering the master's whistle. Iron to a magnet. It touched land like a child's sail boat, nudging, light riding. The monk stooped, picked up the iron, and pounded it back on its handle.

And that beat of metal on wood was the last thing we heard that day. That sound of things finally righting themselves, coming together.

The last thing you heard. No more songs from the feathered Franciscans. We trudged home, and no man's eyes met another's. Something beyond words or song lay on our minds.

15

He let me alone, for a long time, he let me alone. That was his method for making a monk.

With the others he rang many a change. He could be tender, ruthless, explicit (with expletives!), maternal, hard as nails, outgoing, merry, black browed, a thunder head. This was also his method for making monks, or for unmaking unmonks, as the case might be.

He knew how to thin the flock, and did so periodically. He'd come diving into the dove cote like a hawk. And then what feathers and squalls and repentance and intemperate departures!

With me he was different, unfailing in politeness, solicitous even, a rather cool-edged understanding between us, that his door was open, at any time, to explore things further. If and when I wished.

Beyond that, he seemed to sense that I required time. That the wound of birth, and the wound of rebirth, were on me, and would be, and there was no hastening the healing.

And I knew, as he knew, that the wound had been inflicted by his hands, endowed with those fearsome skills which were partly midwife and partly embalmer. And that he had practiced each of those gaudy skills on me.

16

I began to like him, but guardedly.

For months, we were like two dogs, circling one another, sniffing one another's rear end. The eyes start, the heads lower, the dance of approximations, appraisal, sizing up, went on. Some mysterious essence and effluence is in the air; is it fear, is it wariness, or merely a vagrant fart, spelling contempt?

17

There was the episode of the king's leprosy.

We were used to all kinds of people showing up, seeking him out, dragging every human burden to his doorstep.

Some even came to us with a tribute in their jaws, dropped there like a bloody bribe.

In which case, they got more than they bargained on. Bribes; on that subject he was very hell on wheels. I can recall nothing, no sin, no gauche failure, no malice even, that so aroused him. He'd order a corpse hauled away on the litter it arrived in, if he saw so much as a copper on its eyes.

He never brought the subject up with us. I think it a sense of shame that made him keep the subject to himself. It was as though such noisome activities were too obscene to be made an issue among the civilized. Something they used to call "pudor," chastity, a sense that the world and its worldlings would not hesitate for a moment to rape his spirit, to make a whore of his gifts, his uncanny spiritual outreach, his mastery of soul. As though a gift once touched by the world would leave him unclean, violated.

It had something to do, I judged also, with the way he saw himself in God's light. He was borrowing that light, not stealing it. And could you bribe the creator, for his sunlight, for the seasons and vesture of the trees, for the rainfall? Could you buy him off, enrich him, corrupt him? The idea was abominable. He saw himself as part of that freedom, that immunity of God's. And he was. He was free, as God was free. I came to see it, I had to admit it. And I set it down here with a good conscience; his honesty, the free play of his gifts, was not divinely concocted. His strength and purity of soul were his own, won against odds, wrenched from the hands of the unclean, again and again.

And this I came to accept, and be grateful for. This goodness, created out of anger and moral fury and a continuum of conduct which cannot be seized on, either by surprise or calculation.

He wasn't a taxidermist of texts set down by scribes who themselves were fusty with age, their skulls rattling with last year's empty shells. No, he acted in the world, and left the decoding of texts to others (to me?). And better than all his miracles and higher even than his sublime mastery over death, was his honesty—a life that never clouded over, the austere will that never stank of compromise.

———————————— **18** ————————————

To wit. There was a servant who had graduated to a dignity beyond the rest of us. (The Elisean pecking order went from disciple to servant, upward. The servant being more of a friend than the others, admitted closer, as you understand, both to his moods and secrets.)

140

The story is about more than one kind of leprosy.

This servant Giezi had been around a long time. But he was ignorant of the First Rule that governed our household. It was, *you see, but you are also seen.* Giezi was spiritually short of sight, he couldn't discern the other end of those gifts whose fame he basked in, servant of the servant. Dumb as a pike, no more sight that a knot hole in a stick, that was all of him after so many years.

He thought moreover, that he was safe. So he led a second life under his cloak, a life the old man couldn't touch. Or so he thought. And like every sycophant, he had a secret opinion of Eliseus, one he never dared speak. Which was: I despise him. He thought the miracles were a farce in the world, a show (a human benefit for sure, and all that mullarky; but more: oil for an itchy palm). And if the wonder worker was a babe in a thicket, there were others more gifted concerning the world's ways. His task, he said to himself, was to save the child from his own simplicity.

Well, one day we had a distinguished visitor, a sick man. Eliseus received him with courtesy, and cured him with a prayer. Not an unusual morning, one always had the feeling that when generals or princes came in, Eliseus was anxious not to draw things out, courtesy, dispatch. This general of the armies went off with his entourage, back presumably, to more efficient career of butchery than formerly. Eliseus didn't inquire.

It was some time before anyone noticed that Giezi had taken off for the day. Nothing unusual in that, he was a factotum with tenure. What we didn't know, what Eliseus knew, was that the venerable servant's palms were itching like hell, and one might suppose the soles of his feet as well. That he was in fact hoofing after the general. And by the time he caught up with the distinguished beneficiary of the miracle, he had quite a story ready. A story compounded

141

of self-interest, hypocrisy, and a running dog's all but infalli-
ble nose for money.

Greetings from the prophet, he said, warmest greetings.
And bowed. Eliseus has sent me posting after you, with a
most urgent message.

Two young disciples have just arrived from afar, penni-
less and ragged. And the prophet, anxious to relieve such
distress, wonders if you would help—fresh clothing and a
bit of silver to guard against the season. You would?
(Sound of silver crossing palms.) My master's blessing then,
and a blessing from the poor; and may your healing endure
a thousand years.

Was there ever a more inspired piece of quackery? He
bows and bows and backs away, and returns dreaming in his
hustler's heart, of all that silver in his pocket; the end of the
empty hand, empty purse! Garments, olive yards, vineyards, sheep, oxen, men servants, maid servants.

So he came in to us at evening, a glint in eye, a good day,
indeed. A look like a smack of lips, a tradesman's glint, an
edge as of a finely honed bargain, a shaved adversary, a
razor look. And like every cheap winner in the world, an
ignorant mind. Not knowing he's known, not seeing he's
been seen.

And was met with—sublime, deceptively mild, furious as
a sea rising—our master.

——from where do you come, Giezi?
and he lying, dumb as a goat's head
——your servant went nowhere.
and then the storm rising
——was not my heart present, when the man turned back
from his chariot to meet you? So now you have received
money, and received garments, to buy olive yards, and
vineyards and sheep and oxen and men servants and maid
servants!

And the tide was at the craven throat of Giezi and rising.

142

——The leprosy of Naaman shall stick to you, and to your seed forever.

And he went out from him, a leper white as snow.

—————————— **19** ——————————

He took on the world, that man. But he left no Sayings of St. Ecclesiastes, or Miracles of Whoosis the Prophet, or Books of the Big Breathers. Maybe that's what saved him, in his intricate and dangerous game, so like (on the face of it) playing God. He was beyond ego, beyond the siren of history, and the immortal call. Be Immortal! From his skinny shin to his skull, he was one and the same man, one and the same being. He couldn't be bought or sold, is the crude negative unsatisfactory way of saying it. You could run a ream through the middle of him; he wouldn't flinch, it would come out clean. And he'd be standing there dead on his feet. Unattractive, parched, bold, a crystal of God.

Most of our deaths are a coward's cry for mercy. We die as Giezi lived, our ill gotten lives sewn into our rags, death in our heads, silver, silver; we make a living sewing pockets in shrouds. We die of a sickness named possessions. But not this one. Not this one. He fed the hungry and clothed the naked and turned sour water into sweet and made the desert flower and poked into the rancid affairs of kings and generals and recovered lost ax heads and cured lepers.

And for all this, the world could forgive him.

He also inflicted leprosy on the morally leprous and set wild bears on vicious children and spoke crude truths in unwelcome places, played God the father, God the bountiful, even God the judge. And for this latter, of course, the world could never forgive him.

—————————— **20** ——————————

I wandered into his life burdened with an obscure hatred, searching reasons to hate him the more. And so was educated, with what pain, slowly, out of hatred into something like love.

Who, may I ask, ever had better reason to hate another? I had the debt of existence itself against him; after that (as though that were not enough) the life he restored to me. A double debt, infinitely heavy, my unnatural, debt ridden life. All owed to this scrawny raven, this midwife, this voice of tears and woe.

And knew not what to do with my debt. There wasn't a way, you see, to pay off such an IOU. He merely widened those birds' eyes of his, looked at me, blinked like an owl —and waited for the next move, the next word. From me. O he knew how to wait.

And not only wait. He went around the world, saying to the most arrogant as well as the least and last; no, it isn't like that. Or saying in effect, with a slow shake of the head, no, it isn't supposed to be like that.

Or rarely, hardly ever—with a long indrawn breath, as though from regions beyond reach. No, not like that.

He was always comparing us, so to speak, with a world we had no access to. It would have been simple to say, as many did: the world he makes so much of and gives us so much pain about has no existence outside his skull. Or (with an equal fear, I thought) his world never existed, and never will. What people need is not his big stick, his big no, but an "interim ethic." Let's be realistic; let's settle for what decent people can live with here and now. We'll deal with the messiah when his step nears. And by all accounts, he's still a long way off.

―――――――――――― **21** ――――――――――――

There was one thing couldn't be denied, he knew weasel words when he heard them. And as time went on, he helped us recognize them too, and their speakers. We came to see that the world he envisioned was one neither of fantasy nor escape. Nor was it merely God's big scene, empty of human freedom, a locked museum.

No, when you came to the issues he raised in plain language, he was on track all right. Call him ahead of us, call him deeper within us. Or simply call him—sinless. He was sick of sin, as other people grow sick of bad food or an animal's bite or polluted water. He was sick of cruelty and domination and lies and fear of life and its twin, love of death. And he said so, in season and out. And told those who were sick they were sick. And earned no one's gratitude for it.

But more than that. He had something else to offer, a world, himself. Because he was whole, healthy, on his feet, direct of speech, he could speak the truth as he did, meddle where he did, be fearless and longsuffering as he was. He was appalled with those who paid tribute to evil by refusing goodness, who believed in a world that was doomed. As though the contour of a soul was the contour of that world —inescapable, fate, the big folly. No he kept probing, one of those small animals that in freedom, are lithe as quicksilver; and in captivity, beat their brains out against a wall.

He was always calling for more life, as an alcoholic calls for more drink, or a miser for more gold. He wanted everyone to live, he died of life itself, there was no curing him.

Unresigned, before a shape of things most people would merely shrug their shoulders over, and pass on, even if passing on meant stepping over a dead man. Not he. "What shape of things," he'd ask, "and, who gives it shape? And who says the shape of death is not the biggest misshape of all?" So he'd work the dead back into shape. Or, he'd ask, what use is hunger to people, and feed them. And cure leprosy because illness was a wrong, in certain cases. And (infinitely harder to understand) he'd inflict leprosy, on a trusted servant and friend, because such a one had already opened his soul—to leprosy. And he set wild bears against mocking children. (You Christian parents work on that one.) And so on and so on. He left not a stone unturned that his foot touched. He wanted the very stones to take notice, to live.

And crazy and inconsistent and haphazard as it seemed, that life slowly came together, fitted together. It was as though the stones of the road shifted at his passing, into an intricate, even an inspired pattern.

He had another uncommon gift; I want it on the record, if only for my own reflection.

22

I have said in many ways, how clear minded he was, how he read motives, searched the heart, searched the world. For what? For what was there, in the heart, in the world—reality.

The search was its own reward, for himself and those who lived with him, wandered with him, learned from him. They, too, began to sense the subtle interplay of visible and invisible, to whirl now and again in the dance of the universe. Somber as the world was, mindless as its direction seemed, he could always say, that's not all. Something else is at work—at play.

But there were not two worlds, there was one, this was the real news. It was even good news. There was a world of appearances. It claimed to be, announced itself, pressed itself upon you as—the real world. And then within and beyond, lay the invisible, the true shape of things, the undercurrent in whose flow all things moved, came, went, eddied, sank, arose. The springs and source of things. One world. Including a certain ironic self-contrariness, a series of contradictions, of counter claims. He saw it all. You could see that glint, that tiny upstart smile in the mouth behind the hand that both hid and scored his mood.

And especially in the presence of the great, the big ones who beat at his door, being on occasion the most bewildered, taken in shattering surprise, suddenly poor and resourceless, like bronzes cast from their pedestals, when misfortune struck. Gods (in their own estimation) brought low.

23

Like the leper Naaman. He came, in stages so to speak, and loaded with gifts. He'd found his way to Eliseus only by chance. Like one of his prancing horses, he came to us sideways, wild eye, tossing head, a snort for this strange unpromising bundle of wise bones at his feet. Before whom evidently, he must present his own despair and misery. It was quite a story. He had gone first on the word of an Israeli servant girl, to the king of Syria, asking for a letter of introduction to some unknown healer. (He got the word wrong from the start, convinced like most of the rich and great, that only the rich and great hold the keys of life.) The king of Syria eased him on to the king of Samaria who, being a devout believer, was appalled at this gaffe of the pagans; didn't they know that only the Lord healed, etc., etc., and would they have him fall into desperate straits with the almighty, by acting as though he, the king, was a wonderworker, when only the almighty, etc. etc.?

An impasse.

But Eliseus heard of the episode. And with the free self-possession so characteristic of him, he dispatched a message to the king; send the sick man to me. He'll shortly know there's a prophet in Israel.

Eliseus knew who he was, he knew who kings were, he knew who God was. He had no fear of treading that fire. He knew the difference between pride (the stock in trade of kings) and the right mind of the man who, though powerless, is a vessel of divine power.

So his message, surely one of the great utterances of any time. And now see the king's general standing before Eliseus.

Naaman having found the right road at last, and the right man at the end of it, lucky.

Eliseus listened and listened, courteous and patient. He had the greatest skill at listening, he ingested the world through his very pores. And when the general ended, he said, go and bathe seven times in the Jordan.

The general was startled, put down. Weren't there better, cleaner, wider rivers at home? Where was the expected blessing, the laying on of hands, the invocation of the gods? He turned away in disgust. And in weariness, to have come so far, with so many detours, only to be met with so jejune, so absurd an instruction. He cut out.

But a servant, as usual, provided. A servant persuaded the Great Man to follow through, on the principle that though nothing might be gained by such a ceremonial, surely nothing would be lost either?

Naaman went, and bathed, and was healed.

But I want to dwell on that command of Eliseus, another clue to an exalted enigma. Could he not, indeed, have worked the miracle in another way, a more conventional one, one less outrageous to the instincts of the good pagan? Of course, he could.

Why didn't he then?

24

I can only surmise, out of a long series of other episodes. Something about the ironies implicit in faith. Believe, he was saying, and you'll be toppled upside down, like your statues, your ikons, your gods—which in most cases, stand there as symbols of your expectations of the world, of what is due you, of sweet reasonableness and dutiful service from others (from God)—all of which you believe are only your due.

You want to come to faith as you come to honor, as you come to dinner, as you come to a throne; all in reasonable procession, with the pomp and ceremony which translate reality to you—common sense, hierarchy, everything in place. (And above all, your own life secure, free, easy, in control.)

And, of course (Eliseus again) it cannot be. I will not come to you at your summons, to play your spiritual lackey, the slave of God who plays the slave of the general. I will not be your sign that God is also your slave. No. He is God. And I am his servant and not yours; I order you to do such and such an act, ridiculous in the extreme, and humiliating. Go and wash like a slave in ditch water. Wash seven times. Let the world see you, naked and brought low. Let your servants see you in your skin, let them perhaps snicker at the sight, or pity you your disease. Their eyes, pitying or mocking, are your penance and their revenge.

For now the roles are reversed. And this is a very condition and circumstance of faith, of healing.

25

Even in death, he couldn't be done with giving life.

We buried him, with tears. And learned only later, how a funeral procession, passing that spot, had cast their newly dead, for fear of some passing drovers, into the grave of Eliseus. But a greater terror awaited them, for even his bones were quick with God. When the unknown corpse touched his, it recoiled, struck to life. A dead man walked out of the prophet's tomb.